WALKING IN GOD'S GRACE

JESUS CALLING® BIBLE STUDY SERIES

JESUS ALWAYS BIBLE STUDY SERIES

JESUS ALWAYS BIBLE STUDY SERIES

WALKING IN GOD'S GRACE

EIGHT SESSIONS

with Karen Lee-Thorp

THOMAS NELSON
Since 1798

Published in Nashville, Tennessee, by Thomas Nelson. Thomas Nelson is a registered trademark of HarperCollins Christian Publishing, Inc.

All Scripture quotations are taken from The Holy Bible, New International Version®, NIV®. Copyright © 1973, 1978, 1984, 2011 by Biblica, Inc.® Used by permission. All rights reserved worldwide.

ISBN 978-0-310-09137-0

First Printing January 2018 / Printed in the United States of America

CONTENTS

INTRODUCTION

Sometimes our busy and difficult lives give us the impression that God is silent. We cry out to Him, but our feelings tell us He isn't answering our prayers. In this, our feelings are incorrect. God hears the prayers of His children and speaks directly into the situations in which we find ourselves. The trouble is that our lives are often too hectic, our minds too distracted, for us to take in what He offers.

This *Jesus Always* Bible study is designed to help individuals and groups meditate on the words of Scripture and hear them not just as words said to people long ago but as words said to us today in the here and now. The goal is to help the heart open up and respond to what the mind reads—to encounter the living God as He speaks through the Scriptures. The writer to the Hebrews tells us:

> In the past God spoke to our ancestors through the prophets at many times and in various ways, but in these last days he has spoken to us by his Son, whom he appointed heir of all things, and through whom also he made the universe. The Son is the radiance of God's glory and the exact representation of his being, sustaining all things by his powerful word.
>
> —HEBREWS 1:1–3

God has spoken to us through His Son, Jesus Christ. The New Testament gives us the chance to walk with Jesus, see what He does, and hear Him speak into the sometimes-confusing situations in which we find ourselves. The Old Testament tells the story of how God prepared a people to be the family of Jesus, and in the experiences of those men and women, we find our own lives mirrored.

THE GOAL OF THIS SERIES

The *Jesus Always Bible Study Series* offers you a chance to lay down your cares, enter God's Presence, and hear Him speak through His Word. You will get to spend some time silently studying a passage of Scripture, and then, if you're meeting with a group, openly sharing your insights and hearing what others discovered. You'll also get to discuss excerpts from the *Jesus Always* devotional that relate to the themes of the Bible passages. In this way, you will learn how to better make space in your life for the Spirit of God to speak to you through the Word of God and the people of God.

THE FLOW OF EACH SESSION

Each session of this study guide contains the following elements:

- CONSIDER IT. The two questions in this opening section serve as an icebreaker to help you start thinking about the theme of the session, connecting it to your own past or present experience, and allowing you to get to know the others in your group more deeply. If you've had a busy day and your mind is full of distractions, these questions can help you better focus.

- EXPERIENCE IT. Here you will find two readings from *Jesus Always* along with some questions for reflection. This is your chance to talk with others about the biblical principles found within the *Jesus Always* devotions. Can you relate to what each reading describes? What insights from God's Word does it illuminate? What does it motivate you to do? This section will assist you in applying these biblical principles to your everyday habits.

- STUDY IT. Next you'll explore a Scripture passage connected to the session topic and the readings from *Jesus Always*. You will not only analyze these Bible passages but also pray through them in ways designed to engage your heart and your head. You'll first talk with your group about what the verse or verses mean and then spend several minutes in silence, letting God speak into your life through His Word.

- LIVE IT. Finally, you will find five days' worth of suggested Scripture passages that you can pray through on your own during the week. Suggested questions for additional study and reflection are provided.

FOR LEADERS

If you are leading a group through this study guide, please see the Leader's Notes at the end of the guide. You'll find background on the design of the study as well as suggested answers for some of the study questions.

Unearned Grace

CONSIDER IT

In his book *Proof*, Timothy Paul Jones tells the story of his adopted daughter, who had previously spent two years in a different adoptive home. Several times, the previous family had taken all their children except this one girl to Disney World. She had always been left behind with friends. She believed it was always because she did something that deserved punishment. When Jones learned this, he resolved to take this new daughter to Disney World.

However, a month before the trip, the girl began to act up—lying, stealing, and cruelly ridiculing her older sister. She was disciplined each time, but the behavior only became more outrageous. Two days before the trip, after her latest act of mischief, she said, "I know what you're going to do. You're not going to take me to Disney World, are you?"

The young girl, having failed to earn her way into her dream trip several times, was acting in a way that should have placed her as far from the Magic Kingdom as possible. When Jones understood this, he explained that she wasn't going to Disney World because she was good, but because she was part of the family. She was his.[1]

Grace is being treated far better than you deserve. In this session, we will begin to explore grace with a story that shows how completely unearned God's grace is.

1. *When have you received something good that you didn't deserve? How did you respond?*

_____

_____

_____

_____

_____

2. *When you were growing up, did your parents treat you with grace? Explain.*

_____

_____

_____

EXPERIENCE IT

Nurture well your thankfulness, for it is the royal road to Joy! In fact, no pleasure is really complete without expressing gratitude for it. It's good to thank the people through whom you receive blessings, but remember that I am *God from whom all blessings flow*. So praise and thank *Me* frequently each day. This nurtures your soul and completes your Joy. It also enhances your relationship with Me, providing an easy way for you to draw near Me.

As My cherished follower, you have received the glorious gift of grace—unearned, undeserved favor. No one and no set of circumstances can strip you of this lavish gift. You belong to Me forever! *Nothing in all creation will be able to separate you from My Love.*

When you awaken each morning, say, "Thank You, Jesus, for the gift of this new day." As you journey through the day, be on the lookout for blessings and pleasures I scatter along your path. The greatest treasure is My Presence with you, for I am the *indescribable Gift!*

—From *Jesus Always*, June 6

3. *What evidence is there in your life that you have received unearned favor from God?*

_____

_____

_____

4. *How do you respond to God's unearned favor?*

I am *full of grace and truth*. "Grace" refers to the undeserved favor and Love I have for you. Receiving something you don't deserve is humbling, and that's a good thing—protecting you from pride. Grace is a gift of boundless worth, for it secures your eternal salvation. Because you know Me as Savior, I will always be favorable toward you, beloved. My Love for you is undeserved, unearned, and unfailing; so you can't lose it! Just *trust in My unfailing Love, and rejoice in My salvation.*

I am not only full of truth, but *I am the Truth.* People today are barraged by news and messages laced with spin and lies. As a result, cynicism abounds in the world. But in Me and in the Bible, you find absolute, unchanging Truth! Knowing Me *sets your feet on a rock and gives you a firm place to stand.* This secure foundation for your life makes you a bright beacon in a dark, relativistic world. *Let your light shine* so that *many will see and put their trust in Me.*

—FROM *JESUS ALWAYS*, NOVEMBER 12

5. *Do you find that receiving God's grace is humbling? Or do you tend to find yourself taking it for granted or pushing it away because you don't deserve it? Explain.*

6. *How does knowing that God's children can't lose His love make you want to live?*

_____

_____

_____

STUDY IT

Read Matthew 20:1–16. Jesus told this parable to illustrate the outrageousness of God's grace. As you read, note that the story is not meant to be an example of good business practices—rather, it is meant to be shocking to the listeners. Grapes were one of the main crops in Israel, and day laborers (in addition to full-time staff) were needed at harvest time to get them picked before they wilted. A denarius was the normal wage for a laborer who worked all day.

¹ [Jesus said] "For the kingdom of heaven is like a landowner who went out early in the morning to hire workers for his vineyard. ² He agreed to pay them a denarius for the day and sent them into his vineyard.

³ "About nine in the morning he went out and saw others standing in the marketplace doing nothing. ⁴ He told them, 'You also go and work in my vineyard, and I will pay you whatever is right.' ⁵ So they went.

"He went out again about noon and about three in the afternoon and did the same thing. ⁶ About five in the afternoon he went out and found still others standing around. He asked them, 'Why have you been standing here all day long doing nothing?'

⁷ "'Because no one has hired us,' they answered.

"He said to them, 'You also go and work in my vineyard.'

⁸ "When evening came, the owner of the vineyard said to his

foreman, 'Call the workers and pay them their wages, beginning with the last ones hired and going on to the first.'

⁹ "The workers who were hired about five in the afternoon came and each received a denarius. ¹⁰ So when those came who were hired first, they expected to receive more. But each one of them also received a denarius. ¹¹ When they received it, they began to grumble against the landowner. ¹² 'These who were hired last worked only one hour,' they said, 'and you have made them equal to us who have borne the burden of the work and the heat of the day.'

¹³ "But he answered one of them, 'I am not being unfair to you, friend. Didn't you agree to work for a denarius? ¹⁴ Take your pay and go. I want to give the one who was hired last the same as I gave you. ¹⁵ Don't I have the right to do what I want with my own money? Or are you envious because I am generous?'

¹⁶ "So the last will be first, and the first will be last."

7. *In this story, who gets what they don't deserve? Who gets what they do deserve?*

_____

_____

_____

_____

8. *Why are the laborers who are hired first angry? Do you think they have a right to be angry? Explain your view.*

_____

_____

_____

_____

9. *What do you think Jesus meant when He said, "So the last will be first, and the first will be last" (verse 16)?*

_____

_____

_____

10. *Which group of workers do you identify with most: the ones who started working for the landowner early in the day, the ones who were hired in the middle of the day, or the ones who joined in toward the end of the day? Why did you answer the way you did?*

_____

_____

_____

11. *The phrase "are you envious" (verse 15) literally means "is your eye evil?" The "evil eye" covets what belongs to someone else. It keeps laborers from being thankful for their pay because they are blinded by greed for more. Why is envy such a temptation for some of us?*

_____

_____

_____

12. *Take two minutes of silence to reread the passage, looking for a sentence, phrase, or even one word that stands out as something Jesus may want you to* *focus on in your life. If you're meeting with a group, the leader will keep track of time. At the end of two minutes, you may share with the group the word or phrase that came to you in the silence.*

_____

_____

_____

13. *Read the passage aloud again. Take another two minutes of silence, prayerfully considering what response God might want you to make to what you have read in His Word. If you're meeting with a group, the leader will again keep track of time. At the end of two minutes, you may share with the group what came to you in the silence if you wish.*

_____

_____

_____

14. *If you're meeting with a group, how can the members pray for you? If you're using this study on your own, what would you like to say to God right now?*

_____

_____

_____

LIVE IT

At the end of each session you'll find suggested Scripture readings for spending time alone with God during five days of the coming week. This week, the theme of each reading will focus on the idea of grace as a gift from God. Read each passage slowly, pausing to think about what is being said. Rather than approaching this as an assignment to complete, think of it as an opportunity to meet with the One who loves you most. Use any of the questions that are helpful.

Day 1

Read John 4:6–14. This is part of a long encounter between Jesus and a woman who was an outcast in her society. The two meet at a well where the woman is drawing water, at an hour when other people won't be there. "The gift of God" (verse 10) is a gift of God's grace. (The words "grace" and "gift" are related in Greek.) What do you think "living water" means?

How do verses 13–14 further expand on the gift of grace that Jesus is offering?

What are the things for which you thirst?

Today, ask Jesus to quench the thirst you have with His living water.

Day 2

Read Acts 2:36–41. This passage begins with Peter finishing a sermon to a crowd in Jerusalem. What offer of God's grace does he make to the people (see verses 38–39)?

_____

_____

_____

_____

In what way can the Holy Spirit be a gift in your life?

_____

_____

_____

If you've accepted God's gracious offer, what is the evidence of the Holy Spirit in your life?

_____

_____

_____

_____

Thank God today for the gift of the Holy Spirit that He provides to those who follow Him.

Day 3

Read Acts 8:18–23. Simon was a sorcerer in Samaria who saw the power the apostles were able to release in people's lives when they laid hands on them. Why is it important to know that the gift of God can't be bought with money (see verse 20)?

What are some other ways people try to "buy" God's gifts?

Why do you suppose it's hard for some people to simply relax and receive whatever gracious gifts God wants to give them?

Examine your own life today to see if you've unconsciously been trying to "buy" God's gifts.

Day 4

Read Romans 4:3–5. How are wages and gifts different?

Does faith in God earn His favor? Why did you answer the way you did?

What do you think is the connection between grace and faith?

Look for an opportunity today—a grace-filled gift—to exercise faith in God.

Day 5

Read Ephesians 3:7–8. In these verses, Paul describes himself as a servant of the gospel. Did Paul earn or deserve the office God gave him? How can you tell?

_____

_____

_____

Why would Paul think of the responsibility to spread the gospel as a gift of grace?

_____

_____

_____

What grace has God given you that carries with it the responsibility to do something about it?

_____

_____

_____

Look for a chance to live out your gratitude for God's many gifts by giving of yourself today.

NOTES

1. Daniel Montgomery and Timothy Paul Jones, *Proof: Finding Freedom Through the Intoxicating Joy of Irresistible Grace* (Grand Rapids, MI: Zondervan, 2014), 81–84.

OUTRAGEOUS GRACE

CONSIDER IT

Imagine that you are driving well over the speed limit. You're in a hurry to reach your destination, so when a stoplight turns yellow, you speed up to go through it. Unfortunately you've miscalculated, and you end up plowing through a red light and hitting another car. You badly damage this other car and injure the driver.

A police officer has seen the whole event. If the officer decides not to give you a traffic ticket, we would call that *mercy*, because he's not giving you what you completely deserve. But *grace* would go further. It would be God's kind of grace if the driver you have injured volunteers not to notify your insurance companies, promises to pay to have both cars repaired, and even offers to pay for his medical expenses from the accident you caused.

Outrageous? Of course. No sane person would do that. Yet this is what God offers to do for us in Christ. He offers to pay the entire bill for misdeeds that are our fault.

Before Jesus died on the cross, He told stories that were intended to prepare people to understand what He was going to do for them. In this session, we will consider another of these stories as a picture of God's outrageous grace.

1. *Why is the above story of the traffic accident outrageous? What would happen if people made a habit of actions like those of the injured driver?*

_____

_____

_____

2. *What moment of grace—undeserved favor—have you experienced during the past week?*

_____

_____

_____

EXPERIENCE IT

From the fullness of My grace, you have received one blessing after another. Stop for a moment, beloved, and ponder the astonishing gift of salvation—*by grace through faith* in Me. Because it's entirely a gift—*not as a result of works*—this salvation is secure. Your part is just to receive what I accomplished for you on the cross, believing with the faith that was given you. This undeserved Love and favor is yours forever. My grace has infinite value!

Multiple blessings flow out of grace because of its extraordinary fullness. Guilt feelings melt away in the warm Light of My forgiveness. Your identity as a *child of God* gives your life meaning and purpose. Relationships with other people improve as you relate to them with love and forgiveness.

The best response to My bountiful grace is a heart overflowing with gratitude. Take time each day to think about and thank Me for blessings in your life. This protects your heart from weeds of ingratitude that spring up so easily. *Be thankful*!

—FROM *JESUS ALWAYS*, MARCH 10

3. *If you are a Christian, have you experienced feelings of guilt melt away in the light of God's forgiveness? Or do you carry around guilt for things He has forgiven? How does that affect the way you deal with life?*

---

4. *If you are a child of God, does that identity give your life meaning and purpose? Describe how it does or does not change things for you.*

I brought you out into a spacious place. I rescued you because I delighted in you. You are in a spacious place of salvation—saved from being a *slave to sin.* Your salvation is the greatest, most lavish gift you could ever receive. Never stop thanking Me for this infinitely precious gift! In the morning when you awaken, rejoice that I have adopted you into My royal family. Before you go to sleep at night, praise Me for My glorious grace. Live in ways that help others see Me as the fountainhead of abundant, never-ending Life.

I delighted in you, not because of worthiness in you. Rather, I *chose* to delight in you and lavish My Love on you. Since your best efforts could never be sufficient to save you, I clothed you in My own perfect righteousness. Wear this *clothing of salvation* gratefully—with overflowing Joy. Remember that you are royalty in My kingdom, where Glory-Light shines eternally. *Live as a child of Light*, securely robed in radiant righteousness.

—FROM *JESUS ALWAYS*, JANUARY 17

5. *If you are a Christian, what can you do to remind yourself that you have been adopted into God's royal family so the truth of that fact really sinks in?*

_____

_____

_____

6. *How can followers of Christ live in ways that help others see Jesus as the fountainhead of abundant and never-ending life?*

_____

_____

_____

Study It

Read Luke 15:11–32. Jesus told this story to an audience who would have understood that when the younger son asked for his share of the estate, he was effectively telling his father, "I wish you were dead." No son in that culture would have *ever* made such a request to his father, so right from the beginning this story is meant to be shocking. Likewise, a normal father would have had too much dignity to run—much less to greet such a shameful brat. Shoes were a sign of belonging to a prosperous family (slaves went barefoot). The fattened calf was an animal raised for a special occasion, such as a wedding (maybe even for the older son's wedding).

[11] Jesus continued: "There was a man who had two sons. [12] The younger one said to his father, 'Father, give me my share of the estate.' So he divided his property between them.

[13] "Not long after that, the younger son got together all he had, set off for a distant country and there squandered his wealth in wild living. [14] After he had spent everything, there was a severe famine in that whole country, and he began to be in need. [15] So he went and hired himself out to a citizen of that country, who sent him to his fields to feed pigs. [16] He longed to fill his stomach with the pods that the pigs were eating, but no one gave him anything.

[17] "When he came to his senses, he said, 'How many of my father's hired servants have food to spare, and here I am starving to death! [18] I will set out and go back to my father and say to him: Father, I have sinned against heaven and against you. [19] I am no longer worthy to be called your son; make me like one of your hired servants.' [20] So he got up and went to his father.

"But while he was still a long way off, his father saw him and was filled with compassion for him; he ran to his son, threw his arms around him and kissed him.

[21] "The son said to him, 'Father, I have sinned against heaven and against you. I am no longer worthy to be called your son.'

²² "But the father said to his servants, 'Quick! Bring the best robe and put it on him. Put a ring on his finger and sandals on his feet. ²³ Bring the fattened calf and kill it. Let's have a feast and celebrate. ²⁴ For this son of mine was dead and is alive again; he was lost and is found.' So they began to celebrate.

²⁵ "Meanwhile, the older son was in the field. When he came near the house, he heard music and dancing. ²⁶ So he called one of the servants and asked him what was going on. ²⁷ 'Your brother has come,' he replied, 'and your father has killed the fattened calf because he has him back safe and sound.'

²⁸ "The older brother became angry and refused to go in. So his father went out and pleaded with him. ²⁹ But he answered his father, 'Look! All these years I've been slaving for you and never disobeyed your orders. Yet you never gave me even a young goat so I could celebrate with my friends. ³⁰ But when this son of yours who has squandered your property with prostitutes comes home, you kill the fattened calf for him!'

³¹ "'My son,' the father said, 'you are always with me, and everything I have is yours. ³² But we had to celebrate and be glad, because this brother of yours was dead and is alive again; he was lost and is found.'"

7. *What are some of the outrageous things the father does in this story?*

_____

_____

_____

8. *When, if ever, have you been like the younger son in this story, disrespecting and running away from God the Father?*

_____

_____

_____

9. *When, if ever, have you been like the older son?*

10. *How are you called to be like the father in the story?*

11. *The younger son was truly repentant, and he didn't go home taking for granted that he was going to be received back into the family. How is this an important part of the story? What do you think would have happened if his attitude had been different?*

12. *Take two minutes of silence to reread the passage, looking for a sentence, phrase, or even one word that stands out as something Jesus may want you to focus on in your life. If you're meeting with a group, the leader will keep track of time. At the end of two minutes, you may share with the group the word or phrase that came to you in the silence.*

13. *Read the passage aloud again. Take another two minutes of silence, prayerfully considering what response God might want you to make to what you have read in His Word. If you're meeting with a group, the leader will again keep track of time. At the end of two minutes, you may share with the group what came to you in the silence if you wish.*

14. *If you're meeting with a group, how can the members pray for you? If you're using this study on your own, what would you like to say to God right now?*

LIVE IT

This week, each reading will focus on the context for the story that Jesus told of the prodigal son and his older brother. Read each passage slowly, pausing to think about what is being said. Rather than approaching this as an assignment to complete, think of it as an opportunity to meet with the One who loves you most. Use any of the questions that are helpful.

Day 1

Read Luke 15:1–2. These verses describe the situation that prompted Jesus to tell the story about the father and his two sons. Who were meant to see themselves in the character of the older son? Who were meant to see themselves in the younger son?

_____

_____

_____

Why did Jesus welcome sinners and eat with them?

_____

_____

_____

How have you experienced Jesus welcoming you as a sinner? How have you extended that same offer to others in your life?

_____

_____

_____

Today, look for the "sinners" around you, and see if you can find a way to reach out to them.

Day 2

Read Luke 15:3–7. This is the first parable Jesus told in response to the situation described in verses 1–2. Do you think the shepherd was wise to make such a fuss over one lost sheep? Why did you answer the way you did?

_____

_____

_____

How does this story explain why Jesus welcomes sinners and eats with them?

Were you ever like that one lost sheep, or have you been more like the ninety-nine? How does that affect the way you view this story?

Today, if you are one of the ninety-nine, rejoice that you have never been through the bad experiences suffered by the lost ones. And should you heart of a lost one who is found, celebrate that person's return!

Day 3

Read Luke 15:8–10. How is this story like the story of the lost sheep?

Why do you think Jesus felt it necessary to tell three stories to explain to the Pharisees why He spent time with sinners?

Is there a sinner in your life whose repentance would bring you great joy? Who is it?

Today, pray for those who need Jesus in their lives. And if these stories have made you realize your need for Christ, run to Him in prayer and repentance.

Day 4

Read Luke 5:27–28. Tax collectors made their money by collaborating with the hated Roman overlords. They also tended to cheat people. Given this, do you find it surprising that Jesus called one of these men to be His disciple? Why or why not?

How does the passage show that Levi genuinely repented of his sinful life?

In all honesty, would you be comfortable following Jesus alongside someone with a severely corrupt past? Why did you answer the way you did?

Take time today to think about how easy it is for you to show grace to people who have unsavory pasts.

Day 5

Read Luke 5:29–32. Why do you suppose the issue of eating with tax collectors and sinners was such a big deal to the Pharisees?

What did Jesus mean by saying, "It is not the healthy who need a doctor" (verse 31)?

Did the Pharisees need grace? Why or why not?

Ask Jesus today to show you how to reach out to the "spiritually sick" and show them hospitality.

RESCUING GRACE

CONSIDER IT

In her memoir, *In My Father's House*, Gabrielle Carey describes the crushing weight she lived under as a young woman with her atheist father in Western Australia:

> One of the hardest aspects of growing up as the daughter of a humanist was the worry of having to live up to incredibly high intellectual and moral standards. And worse, what happened when it was discovered that you hadn't? Would you be given a second chance? Could you confess your weaknesses? Would you ever be forgiven? What would my father say if he found out that I was just another brainless, mind-molded, media-manipulated failure to humanity?[1]

Eventually, Carey went to Ireland, where she was drawn to the Christian faith because it offered her chances at confession and forgiveness.

In this session, we'll look at the story of another woman—one who was badly in need of forgiveness because of the mistakes she had made in the past. We'll see how a gift of grace from God rescued her from the legalistic punishment of hypocrites and blessed her with a fresh start.

1. *What are the benefits of having high moral standards?*

_____

_____

_____

2. *What are the potential drawbacks of having high moral standards? How can you potentially avoid these drawbacks?*

_____

_____

_____

EXPERIENCE IT

I rejoice over you with singing. Open wide your heart, mind, and spirit to receive My richest blessings. Because you are My blood-bought child, My Love for you flows continuously from *the throne of grace.* Look up and receive all that I have for you. Listen and hear Me singing songs of Joy because of My *great delight in you.* You can approach Me boldly—with confidence—trusting that you are indeed *the one I love.*

The world teaches you that love is conditional: based on performance, appearance, and status. Even though you don't believe this lie, the constant onslaught of this message in the media can penetrate your thinking. That's why it is so important to spend time focusing on Me—soaking in My Presence, absorbing My Word.

Setting aside time to be alone with Me is countercultural, so this practice requires discipline and determination. However, it is well worth the effort. Living close to Me brightens your life immeasurably. *With Me is the fountain of Life; in My Light you see Light.*

—FROM *JESUS ALWAYS*, MARCH 14

3. *What are some of the ways the world sends you the message that love is conditional?*

---

4. *What helps you know that you can approach the throne of grace for forgiveness?*

You are troubled by fear of failure, but My Love for you will never fail. Let Me describe what I see as I gaze at you, beloved. You look regal, for I have clothed you in My righteousness and *crowned you with glory and honor*. You *are radiant*, especially when you are looking at Me. You are beautiful as you *reflect My Glory* back to Me. In fact, you delight Me so much that *I rejoice over you with shouts of Joy*! This is how you appear through My grace-filled vision.

Because I am infinite, I can see you as you are now and as you will be in heaven—simultaneously. Viewing you in the present, I work with you on things you need to change. Seeing you from the heavenly perspective, I love you as if you were already perfect.

I want you to learn to look at yourself—and others—through the lens of My unfailing Love. As you persevere in this, you will gradually find it easier to love yourself *and* others.

—FROM *JESUS ALWAYS*, APRIL 27

5. *If you have accepted Christ as your Savior, how easy is it for you to see yourself through God's grace-filled vision? Explain.*

6. *When God works with you on things in your life that need to change, does that feel to you like a grace-filled process or one that makes you feel condemned?*

STUDY IT

Read John 8:2–11. The Pharisees and religious leaders set up the situation described in this passage to have evidence with which to accuse Jesus. Note that under the law, if this woman was caught in the act of adultery, there had to be two witnesses present. The man should have been arrested as well, but the religious leaders let him go free. They thought they had Jesus in a dilemma: if He opposed the stoning of the woman, He would prove Himself opposed to what the Bible said about punishing adultery (see Deuteronomy 22:23–24). However, if He agreed to the woman's stoning, He would betray the compassion for which He was widely known.

² At dawn he [Jesus] appeared again in the temple courts, where all the people gathered around him, and he sat down to teach them. ³ The teachers of the law and the Pharisees brought in a woman caught in adultery. They made her stand before the group ⁴ and said to Jesus, "Teacher, this woman was caught in the act of adultery. ⁵ In the Law Moses commanded us to stone such women. Now what do you say?" ⁶ They were using this question as a trap, in order to have a basis for accusing him.

But Jesus bent down and started to write on the ground with his finger. ⁷ When they kept on questioning him, he straightened up and said to them, "Let any one of you who is without sin be the first to throw a stone at her." ⁸ Again he stooped down and wrote on the ground.

⁹ At this, those who heard began to go away one at a time, the older ones first, until only Jesus was left, with the woman still standing there. ¹⁰ Jesus straightened up and asked her, "Woman, where are they? Has no one condemned you?"

¹¹ "No one, sir," she said.

"Then neither do I condemn you," Jesus declared. "Go now and leave your life of sin."

7. *How do the Pharisees and teachers of the law treat the woman in this scene?*

8. *How does Jesus treat the woman in this scene?*

9. *Do you think Jesus is too easy on the woman and her sin? Why did you answer the way you did?*

10. *In verse 7, Jesus says, "Let any one of you who is without sin be the first to throw a stone at her." Jesus knows these religious teachers are all hypocrites in the way they have brought this case—and they know that He knows it. Based on Jesus' example, how should the church deal with sins like this by its members?*

11. *Jesus doesn't condemn the woman, but he does hold her accountable. How are these two concepts different?*

12. *Take two minutes of silence to reread the passage, looking for a sentence, phrase, or even one word that stands out as something Jesus may want you to focus on in your life. If you're meeting with a group, the leader will keep track of time. At the end of two minutes, you may share with the group the word or phrase that came to you in the silence.*

13. *Read the passage aloud again. Take another two minutes of silence, prayerfully considering what response God might want you to make to what you have read in His Word. If you're meeting with a group, the leader will again keep track of time. At the end of two minutes, you may share with the group what came to you in the silence if you wish.*

14. *If you're meeting with a group, how can the members pray for you? If you're using this study on your own, what would you like to say to God right now?*

LIVE IT

This week, the theme of each reading will focus on forgiveness. Read each passage slowly, pausing to think about what is being said. Rather than approaching this as an assignment to complete, think of it as an opportunity to meet with the One who loves you most. Use any of the questions that are helpful.

Day 1

1. *Read 1 Kings 8:33–36. This is part of King Solomon's prayer at the dedication of the temple in Jerusalem. What does Solomon say the people need to do to receive God's forgiveness?*

What were some of the people's negative experiences that signaled to them that they were in need of repentance and forgiveness?

Do you think experiences such as these are always or usually a signal that
someone has sin that needs repentance? Why did you answer the way you did?

_____

_____

_____

_____

Thank God today that He doesn't leave His children stuck in the consequences of their sins—but provides a way for forgiveness.

Day 2

Read 2 Chronicles 7:13–15. This passage is similar to the one on Day 1, but
it adds the invitation to humble yourself before God. Why is humility so
important in repentance and forgiveness?

_____

_____

_____

_____

How do you go about humbling yourself?

_____

_____

_____

_____

This passage is a promise for a community (a nation), not for an individual. How does that affect the way you apply it to your own situation?

Humble yourself before God about the sins of your community or nation—the sins in which you share responsibility.

Day 3

Read Psalm 32:1–5. How did the psalmist suffer before he confessed his sin?

Have you ever suffered with unconfessed sin? If so, what was that like for you?

If being forgiven is such an experience of blessing, why do you suppose followers of Christ still often hold back from confessing?

Spend some time today searching your heart to see if there is any sin that you need to confess.

Day 4

Read Matthew 6:9–15. These are Jesus' instructions for how to pray. Like the earlier passages, He makes forgiveness conditional. God will forgive us if we do something else (like repenting and humbling ourselves). In this case, what is the condition under which our Father will forgive us (see verse 14)?

Does this condition surprise you? Why did you answer the way you did?

Who, if anyone, do you need to forgive today? (Take some time to give that some thought.)

As you go through your day, keep this thought at the front of your mind: *Is there anyone I need to forgive?*

Day 5

Read Matthew 18:21–35. How do you respond to the idea of forgiving someone seventy-seven times (see verse 22), which really implies an unlimited number of times? Why?

What is the point of the parable that Jesus tells? What does it tell you about yourself?

How easy is it for you to forgive others? Are you harboring the desire for someone to pay for what they did? Explain.

Be honest about your feelings toward anyone who has wronged you. Instead of swallowing the anger, tell God the truth about it and ask for His help to truly forgive.

NOTES

1. Gabrielle Carey, *In My Father's House* (Tuggerah, New South Wales: Pan Macmillan, 1992).

SACRIFICING GRACE

CONSIDER IT

Atonement. It's one of those thousand-dollar words whose meaning is only a vague notion for many people. But the idea of atonement lies at the heart of God's grace. It means "reconciliation" or "satisfaction paid to an offended party."

The Old Testament describes an annual Day of Atonement that vividly illustrates the concept. Once each year, the high priest took two goats from the herds and presented them to the Lord. One of them was considered the scapegoat. The high priest would place his hands on this animal, symbolically laying all the sins of the people on it, and then the goat would be driven into the wilderness, carrying the people's sins away with it. The second goat was sacrificed, and the high priest would sprinkle some of its blood on the Ark of the Covenant in the temple. The blood made atonement for the people because of their sins.

Jesus' death was a once-for-all-time sacrifice of atonement. He took the place of the two goats in wiping away the people's sins. In this session, we'll consider what difference it makes to us that Jesus became the sacrifice of atonement for all who would receive Him.

1. *How do you react to this idea of a blood sacrifice being necessary to wipe away sins?*

2. *How old were you when you were first exposed to the idea of Jesus dying for your sins? What did it mean to you at that time?*

EXPERIENCE IT

Rejoice that *I have clothed you with garments of salvation*. This *robe of righteousness* is yours forever and ever! Because I am your Savior, My perfect righteousness can never be taken away from you. This means you don't need to be afraid to face your sins—or to deal with them. As you become aware of sin in your life, confess it and receive My forgiveness in full measure.

It is essential also to forgive yourself. Self-hatred is not pleasing to Me, and it is very unhealthy for you. I urge you to take many looks at *Me* for every look at your sins or failures. I am the perfect antidote to the poison of self-loathing.

Since you are already precious in My sight, you don't have to prove your worth by trying to be good enough. I lived a perfect life on your behalf because I knew that you could not. Now I want you to live in the glorious freedom of being My fully forgiven follower. Remember that *there is no condemnation for those who belong to Me*.

—FROM *JESUS ALWAYS*, FEBRUARY 6

3. *Why don't followers of Christ need to be afraid to face their sins (see 1 John 1:9)?*

4. *Why don't they need to dwell on their past failures and sins they have confessed to God?*

Thank Me joyfully for forgiving *all* your sins—past, present, and future; known and unknown. Forgiveness is your greatest need, and I have met that need perfectly—forever! I am *the eternal Life that was with the Father and has appeared to you.* Because you believe in Me as your Savior-God, you have *everlasting Life.* Let this amazing promise fill you with Joy and drive out fear of the future. Your future is glorious and secure: *an inheritance that can never perish, spoil, or fade—kept in heaven for you.* The best response to this priceless, infinite gift is gratitude!

The more frequently you thank Me, the more joyful your life will be. So be on the lookout for things that fuel your gratitude. The very act of thanking Me—in spoken or written word, in silent prayers, whispers, shouts, or songs of praise—increases your Joy and lifts you above your circumstances. A delightful way to express your adoration is reading psalms out loud. Rejoice in Me, My redeemed one, for *nothing can separate you from My Love.*

—From *Jesus Always*, May 29

5. *How do you typically respond when you consider that God has forgiven all His children's sins? Is this something that's real for you, or is it more of an idea you believe but don't experience?*

6. *What are some of the benefits of practicing gratitude for forgiveness?*

Study It

Read Romans 3:21–26. This is an excerpt from Paul's long explanation of the good news about Jesus. As you read, note that *righteousness* is the action by which God puts people into right relationship with Him. He does this for those who put their trust in what Jesus has done. *Redemption* is buying a slave out of slavery (in this case, slavery to sin, death, and Satan). A *sacrifice of atonement* is the fulfillment of all the Old Testament sacrifices, when an animal would symbolically pay the death penalty deserved by people. Jesus paid the death penalty we earned when we rebelled against God, and He *justifies* all who receive Him by putting them into a right relationship with God.

> [21] But now apart from the law the righteousness of God has been made known, to which the Law and the Prophets testify. [22] This righteousness is given through faith in Jesus Christ to all who believe. There is no difference between Jew and Gentile, [23] for all have sinned and fall short of the glory of God, [24] and all are justified freely by his grace through the redemption that came by Christ Jesus. [25] God presented Christ as a sacrifice of atonement, through the shedding of his blood—to be received by faith. He did this to demonstrate his righteousness, because in his forbearance he had left the sins committed beforehand unpunished—[26] he did it to demonstrate his righteousness at the present time, so as to be just and the one who justifies those who have faith in Jesus.

7. *Jesus' death on the cross was the ultimate sacrifice of atonement (see verse 25). How was this an act of grace?*

8. *How do sinners acquire righteousness? How is this a gift of grace?*

9. *Why couldn't God just forget all the sins people committed? Why was Jesus' death required to uphold God's justice?*

10. *If you have accepted Christ, you have been justified—made righteous. In God's eyes, you are perfectly righteous, even though He isn't blind to your faults. How do you live out this right relationship with God?*

11. *Jesus offers to redeem you from slavery to sin and death. If you have accepted this gift, how has it affected your view of death?*

12. *Take two minutes of silence to reread the passage, looking for a sentence, phrase, or even one word that stands out as something Jesus may want you to focus on in your life. If you're meeting with a group, the leader will keep track* *of time. At the end of two minutes, you may share with the group the word or phrase that came to you in the silence.*

---

13. *Read the passage aloud again. Take another two minutes of silence, prayerfully considering what response God might want you to make to what you have read in His Word. If you're meeting with a group, the leader will again keep track of time. At the end of two minutes, you may share with the group what came to you in the silence if you wish.*

---

14. *If you're meeting with a group, how can the members pray for you? If you're using this study on your own, what would you like to say to God right now?*

LIVE IT

This week, each reading will focus on a portion of Leviticus 16, where the instructions for the Day of Atonement are described. Read each passage slowly, pausing to think about what is being said. Rather than approaching this as an assignment to complete, think of it as an opportunity to meet with the One who loves you most. Use any of the questions that are helpful.

Day 1

Read Leviticus 16:1–5. According to verse 2, why will the priest die if he goes into the Most Holy Place whenever he wants? What does that say about the effect God's presence had on people before the time of Jesus?

Bathing and putting on sacred clothing were symbols of purifying the priest from the sinful state of ordinary humans. What does this say about our status before God apart from the death of Christ?

What do you think it would have been like to constantly offer blood sacrifices for your sins in order to approach God?

Thank Jesus today for offering to be your sin offering and your guilt offering.

Day 2

Read Leviticus 16:6–14. Aaron, the high priest, had to burn incense before the Ark of the Covenant because it represented God's earthly throne and His presence was there. Without the cloud of incense, Aaron would have died if he had looked straight at the place above the Ark where God was present (see verse 13). What does this suggest about people's ability to enjoy God's presence in those days?

Why did Aaron have to offer the bull for himself before he offered the sacrifice for the people (see verse 6)? What does this say about the difference between Aaron as the Israelites' high priest and Jesus as the high priest of His people?

Aaron sprinkled some of the blood from the bull onto the lid of the Ark. This was known as the "atonement cover" (verse 14, or "mercy seat" in the KJV and ESV). Why do you think it was given this name?

Praise Jesus today for being the perfect high priest who has full access to the Father's throne of grace.

Day 3

Read Leviticus 16:15–19. Why did the high priest have to sprinkle the blood onto the atonement cover every year?

_____

_____

_____

_____

What does that say about the people and the system of sacrifices?

_____

_____

_____

_____

Aaron even had to make atonement for the altar on which the daily sacrifices were offered throughout the year. What impression of God's holiness does all this build up in your mind?

_____

_____

_____

_____

Thank Jesus that He has offered a once-for-all-time sacrifice that never has to be repeated because it was perfect and permanent.

Day 4

Read Leviticus 16:20–22. What happened to the live goat?

What was the point of the live goat?

How did Jesus take the place of the live goat, just as he took the place of the priest and the sacrificed animals?

Praise Jesus today for His offer to be the scapegoat for your sins.

Day 5

Read Leviticus 16:29–31. You've read what the priest did on the Day of Atonement. What do these verses now say about what the people did on this day?

What was the point of the people's actions on this day?

_____

_____

_____

What is the value for Christians in understanding the Day of Atonement?

_____

_____

_____

Today, look for a way to pay tribute to Jesus for His sacrifice of atonement for sin.

GLORIOUS GRACE

CONSIDER IT

The eighteenth-century preacher Jonathan Edwards once gave a sermon called "Glorious Grace." In this sermon, he argued that God's decision to rescue humanity after Adam's fall was pure grace and not motivated by any need on God's side. Edwards pointed out that God didn't need us or our praise. He was already full of happiness and already had tens of thousands of angels to praise Him (and if that wasn't enough, He could easily have made creatures more perfect than us to eternally sing His praises).

So, given this, why *did* God set out on a plan that would prove to be so costly to Himself in order to buy His creation back from the sinful slavery into which they sold themselves? The answer is simple: purely because He was overflowing with love for His creation and chose to do so! It is His nature to be unfailingly generous.

In this session, we will delve into the apostle Paul's hymn to God's glorious grace and learn what makes it so glorious. We will revel in the benefits that God has offered to us in Christ and see if they can move us to security and gratitude.

1. *Where have you seen God's grace at work in the past week?*

2. *How have you been invited to respond to grace in the past week?*

EXPERIENCE IT

I approve of you, My child. Because you are Mine—adopted into My royal family—I see you through eyes of grace. *I chose you before the creation of the world to be holy and blameless in My sight.* I know you fall short of this perfect standard in your daily living. But I *view* you as holy and blameless because this is your permanent position in My kingdom. Of course, I don't endorse everything you do (or fail to do). Still, I approve of *you*—your true self, the one I created you to be.

I know how much you long for My affirmation—and how hard it is for you to accept it. I want you to learn to see yourself and others through grace-vision. Looking through eyes of grace, you can focus more on what is good and right than on what is bad and wrong. You learn to cooperate with Me and embrace what I'm doing in your life: *transforming you into My likeness with ever-increasing Glory.* I not only *approve* of you, I *delight* in you!

—FROM *JESUS ALWAYS*, JUNE 1

3. *If you are a child of God, what difference does it make to you that God approves of you?*

_____

_____

_____

_____

4. *Why do you think God's affirmation is often hard to accept?*

_____

_____

_____

As you journey through life with Me, see the hope of heaven shining on your path—lighting up your perspective. Remember that you are one of My *chosen people, belonging to Me. I called you out of darkness into My wonderful Light.* Savor the richness of these concepts: *I chose you before the creation of the world,* so nothing can separate you from Me. You belong to Me forever! I drew you out of the darkness *of sin and death* into the exquisite Light of eternal Life.

The brightness of My Presence helps you in multiple ways. The closer to Me you live, the more clearly you can see the way forward. As you soak in this Love-drenched Light, *I give you strength and bless you with Peace.* My radiance blesses not only you but also other people as it permeates your whole being. This time spent focusing on Me helps you become more like Me, enabling you to shine into the lives of others. I'm continually drawing My loved ones out of darkness into My glorious Light.

—FROM *JESUS ALWAYS*, DECEMBER 9

5. *What does the Bible mean when it says that God is "light"? How does that affect you?*

_____

_____

_____

_____

6. *God's radiance comes to believers as a gift of God's grace. Why is this important to keep in mind?*

_____

_____

_____

STUDY IT

Read Ephesians 1:3–10. In this passage, Paul outlines the wondrous things God has done for us through the life, death, and resurrection of His Son. To be *holy* is to be set apart as pure for a special purpose. "Adoption to sonship" alludes to Roman law regarding inheritances. Families didn't adopt babies the way we do today; instead, an older man without a biological heir often adopted a young man to be his legal heir. The adopted son took on all of the adult rights and responsibilities that he would have held if he had been a biological heir. A young woman was never adopted in this way under Roman law, but Paul applies "adoption to sonship" to his female readers as well as his male ones.

> [3] Praise be to the God and Father of our Lord Jesus Christ, who has blessed us in the heavenly realms with every spiritual blessing in Christ. [4] For he chose us in him before the creation of the world to be holy and blameless in his sight. In love [5] he predestined us for adoption to sonship through Jesus Christ, in accordance with his pleasure and will—[6] to the praise of his glorious grace, which he has freely given us in the One he loves. [7] In him we have redemption through his blood, the forgiveness of sins, in accordance with the riches of God's grace [8] that he lavished on us. With all wisdom and understanding, [9] he made known to us the mystery of his will according to his good pleasure, which he purposed in Christ, [10] to be put into effect when the times reach their fulfillment—to bring unity to all things in heaven and on earth under Christ.

7. *One of Paul's favorite phrases was "in Christ" or "in him" (verses 3, 4, 7, 9). It's as if Christ were a country to which His followers had transferred their citizenship. What are some of the blessings you are offered if you are "in Christ"?*

8. *In the heavenly Father's eyes, His children are considered holy and blameless (see verse 4). How does that affect the way you treat yourself?*

_____

_____

_____

_____

9. *How does your adoption as God's heir affect you if you have accepted this gift?*

_____

_____

_____

_____

10. *How are all these blessings examples of God's "glorious grace" (verse 6)?*

_____

_____

_____

_____

11. *What comes to mind when you read that Jesus will "bring unity to all things in heaven and on earth" (verse 10)? What does this mean to you?*

_____

_____

_____

_____

12. *Take two minutes of silence to reread the passage, looking for a sentence, phrase, or even one word that stands out as something Jesus may want you to focus on in your life. If you're meeting with a group, the leader will keep track of time. At the end of two minutes, you may share with the group the word or phrase that came to you in the silence.*

13. *Read the passage aloud again. Take another two minutes of silence, prayerfully considering what response God might want you to make to what you have read in His Word. If you're meeting with a group, the leader will again keep track of time. At the end of two minutes, you may share with the group what came to you in the silence if you wish.*

14. *If you're meeting with a group, how can the members pray for you? If you're using this study on your own, what would you like to say to God right now?*

LIVE IT

This week, the theme of each reading will focus on God's glory. Read each passage slowly, pausing to think about what is being said. Rather than approaching this as an assignment to complete, think of it as an opportunity to meet with the One who loves you most. Use any of the questions that are helpful.

Day 1

Read Exodus 16:10 and 24:16–17. When you think about God's glorious grace, it's important to pause and consider what God's glory is. What did "the glory of the Lord" mean at the time when the Lord was freeing His people from slavery in Egypt and leading them into the Promised Land?

What did "the glory of the Lord" look like when God was confirming His covenant with Moses on Mount Sinai?

How is your mental picture of the glory of God's grace enhanced by thinking of the way God manifested Himself physically for the Israelites in the desert?

Praise God for His glorious presence with His people through the ages, right to this very day.

Day 2

Read Exodus 33:18–23 and 34:5–7. What happened when Moses prayed to see God's glory?

_____

_____

_____

_____

What do you learn about God from the fact that Moses could be shown His "back" but not His "face"?

_____

_____

_____

_____

What else do you learn about God from what He says in Exodus 34:6–7?

_____

_____

_____

_____

Praise God today for His awe-inspiring "otherness"—and for nonetheless desiring to show His glory to His children through His grace.

59

Day 3

Read John 1:14. According to this verse, how did God reveal His glory?

_____

_____

_____

How was this revelation of God's glory connected to the fiery cloud of glory in the Old Testament? How was it different?

_____

_____

_____

What did grace have to do with this manifestation of God's glory?

_____

_____

_____

Thank Jesus today for becoming flesh and dwelling among us.

Day 4

Read John 17:1–5. Jesus said this prayer on the evening before He gave His life for sinful humankind. What did He specifically ask God to do?

_____

_____

_____

In verse 4, Jesus says, "I have brought you glory on earth by finishing the work you gave me to do." What was that work?

_____

_____

_____

In verse 5, Jesus speaks of "the glory I had with you before the world began." What do you know about that glory from earlier passages you've studied?

_____

_____

_____

Glorify Jesus today by praising Him for offering His life for you in the supreme act of grace.

Day 5

Read John 12:23–28. According to verses 23–24, how was Jesus about to be glorified? Why was this necessary?

_____

_____

_____

According to verses 27–28, how did Jesus deal with a troubled soul? Why was His soul troubled?

_____

_____

_____

Why do you suppose Jesus talked of His death as something that would bring glory to Him and to His Father?

Look for a way to bring glory to God today by doing His will.

SAVING GRACE

CONSIDER IT

The great painter Pablo Picasso, who revolutionized the art world, entered a frenzy of painting late in life because he couldn't endure the hard truth that his best work was behind him. Nothing could negate the abyss of approaching death. He was frantic, desperate, and helpless.

However, because of Jesus, that doesn't have to be our destiny. In this session, we're going to look at an amazing snapshot of the contrast between life without Jesus and life with Him. Without Him, we're mired in the worst aspects of our world, wildly trying to string together moments of satisfaction in a life with very little meaning (see Ecclesiastes 1:1–11). With Him, we have the opportunity to do things that are genuinely of value that will last for eternity.

Life without God leads to all kinds of dysfunction—greed, striving for wealth and success, broken families, addiction, injustice, hoarding . . . the list of ills is endless. However, life with God transcends all these things, offering the hope of healing. And how do we get that precious life? By grace, of course. Always by grace.

1. *Think of someone you know who doesn't believe in Jesus but who lives a basically decent life. Is it hard for you to think of this person's life as ultimately futile? Why or why not?*

---

2. *If Pablo Picasso reflects a secular person's response to impending death, what would be a Christian response to the approach of death?*

EXPERIENCE IT

Proclaim My salvation day after day. You need to recall the truth of the gospel every single day: *By grace you have been saved through faith, and this is not your own doing; it's a gift—not a result of works.* This truth is very countercultural. The world tells you that you have to work at being good enough. Your own fallen mind and heart will agree with these messages unless you are vigilant. That's why Scripture warns you to be *alert.* The devil is the *accuser* of My followers. His accusations discourage and defeat many Christians, so remind yourself of gospel-truth frequently.

The best response to the glorious gift of grace is a thankful heart that delights in doing My will. It is vital to proclaim the gospel not only to yourself but to the world. *Declare My Glory to the nations!* Seek to share this good news—both near (to family, friends, coworkers) and far (to the nations). *All peoples* need to know the truth about Me. Let your thankfulness motivate you, energize you, and fill you with Joy!

—FROM *JESUS ALWAYS,* JULY 16

3. *Why would it be a good idea for Christians to remind themselves of the truth of salvation every day?*

---

4. *If you have accepted this glorious gift of grace, in what ways should it motivate and energize your conversations with those who aren't believers?*

I am *the One and Only who came from the Father, full of grace and truth.* I came from Him and I returned to Him because I am God—the second Person of the Trinity.

I entered your world to provide a way for you to have a living, eternal relationship with your Father-God. People who do not know Me have often stated that there are many ways to God. But this claim is absolutely untrue: *I am the Way, the Truth, and the Life. No one comes to the Father except through Me.*

I come to *you*, beloved, *full of grace.* Because you have trusted Me to save you from your sins through My sacrificial death on the cross, you have nothing to fear. You don't need to dread failure or performing below expectations. Since I am your Savior—and you cannot save yourself—your security rests in My grace. Rejoice that I am both faithful and sufficient. In spite of all the trouble in this world, *in Me you may have Peace. I have overcome the world!*

—FROM *JESUS ALWAYS*, APRIL 23

5. *What do you think it means to say that Jesus is "full of grace"?*

_____

_____

_____

_____

6. *Do you dread failure or performing below expectations? How would this dread affect a person's behavior?*

_____

_____

_____

_____

STUDY IT

Read Ephesians 2:1–10. Paul's intent in this passage is to contrast what was formerly true of God's children against what is now true of them. They used to be dead—spiritually dead, having an empty life hardly worth living—but now they are fully alive to God, to themselves, and to other people. As you read, note that "the ruler of the kingdom of the air" refers to Satan. "This world" (verse 2) means the systems by which this world's sin-riddled institutions run. Likewise, our "flesh" (verse 3) does not refer to our physical bodies but rather to our lower natures—the part of us that has selfish desires and is hostile to allowing God to run our lives.

[1] As for you, you were dead in your transgressions and sins, [2] in which you used to live when you followed the ways of this world and of the ruler of the kingdom of the air, the spirit who is now at work in those who are disobedient. [3] All of us also lived among them at one time, gratifying the cravings of our flesh and following its desires and thoughts. Like the rest, we were by nature deserving of wrath. [4] But because of his great love for us, God, who is rich in mercy, [5] made us alive with Christ even when we were dead in transgressions—it is by grace you have been saved. [6] And God raised us up with Christ and seated us with him in the heavenly realms in Christ Jesus, [7] in order that in the coming ages he might show the incomparable riches of his grace, expressed in his kindness to us in Christ Jesus. [8] For it is by grace you have been saved, through faith—and this is not from yourselves, it is the gift of God—[9] not by works, so that no one can boast. [10] For we are God's handiwork, created in Christ Jesus to do good works, which God prepared in advance for us to do.

7. *If you are a Christian, what do you remember about the time when you were dead in your sins (see verses 1–2)?*

_____

_____

_____

8. *Illicit sex is an obvious craving of the flesh, but what are some other things the flesh craves (see verse 3)?*

_____

_____

_____

_____

9. *What does it mean to be saved by grace (see verse 5)?*

_____

_____

_____

_____

10. *What role does faith play in a believer's salvation (see verses 6–8)?*

_____

_____

_____

_____

11. *What role do good works have in the lives of people saved by grace (see verses 9–10)?*

_____

_____

_____

_____

12. *Take two minutes of silence to reread the passage, looking for a sentence, phrase, or even one word that stands out as something Jesus may want you to focus on in your life. If you're meeting with a group, the leader will keep track of time. At the end of two minutes, you may share with the group the word or phrase that came to you in the silence.*

13. *Read the passage aloud again. Take another two minutes of silence, prayerfully considering what response God might want you to make to what you have read in His Word. If you're meeting with a group, the leader will again keep track of time. At the end of two minutes, you may share with the group what came to you in the silence if you wish.*

14. *If you're meeting with a group, how can the members pray for you? If you're using this study on your own, what would you like to say to God right now?*

LIVE IT

This week, the theme of each reading will focus on the good works that God's people can do for His kingdom. Read each passage slowly, pausing to think about what is being said. Rather than approaching this as an assignment to complete, think of it as an opportunity to meet with the One who loves you most. Use any of the questions that are helpful.

Day 1

Read John 6:27–29. What is the work that God "requires" for salvation?

_____

_____

_____

What does it mean to believe in Jesus? Is it enough to believe things about Him, such as that He is the Son of God who became a man and rose from the dead? Explain.

_____

_____

_____

Why do you suppose it's so ingrained in some people to constantly work harder to attain a right relationship with God?

_____

_____

_____

If you have chosen to follow Christ, express your belief in Him today with concrete words.

Day 2

Read Romans 9:31–33. What did the people of Israel do wrong in their effort to have a right relationship with God?

In what way can this become a stumbling stone?

Has this ever been a stumbling stone for you? Why did you answer the way you did?

Today, be aware of the temptation to believe you are closer to God when you do something good—and thank God again that His grace comes as a free gift that can't be earned.

Day 3

Read Romans 3:20. What was the purpose of the Law in the Old Testament?

Have God's commandments ever helped you become aware of your sin? If so, give an example.

_____

_____

_____

_____

If the laws in Scripture haven't helped you become aware of your sin, what has helped you? Why is that a useful part of the spiritual life?

_____

_____

_____

_____

_____

Ask God to help you become aware of any sin in your life today.

Day 4

Read John 14:11–12. In this passage, Jesus talks about good works in a very different way. What does Jesus say about good works?

_____

_____

_____

_____

Jesus' works included miracles as well as acts of service, humility, and love. What do you think it means to say that ordinary believers will do greater works than He did?

What works do you think the Holy Spirit wants to do through you if you are a follower of Christ? Be specific.

Look for an opportunity to do a work of service in Jesus' name today.

Day 5

Read James 2:14–19. How does James describe the connection between faith and good deeds?

What do you think James means when he says, "faith by itself, if it is not accompanied by action, is dead" (verse 17)?

_____

_____

_____

_____

How can believers in Christ demonstrate their faith by their deeds? Give a couple of examples.

_____

_____

_____

_____

If you are a follower of Christ, look for an opportunity today to demonstrate that faith through action.

TRANSFORMING GRACE

CONSIDER IT

Robert Louis Stevenson once wrote a tale of a gifted doctor named Dr. Jekyll, a likeable man, who harbored hidden longings to do wicked things. He invented a serum that, when swallowed, allowed him to transform into a younger man utterly without conscience: Mr. Hyde. In this way, he could do all his acts of evil as *Hyde* and all his acts of goodness as *Jekyll*. Tragically, however, the doctor lost control and found himself transforming into Hyde without the serum. Eventually, he was unable to turn back into Jekyll, even with the help of the serum.

The story of Dr. Jekyll and Mr. Hyde has captivated readers for generations. Perhaps this is because each of us resonates with this internal conflict. We too have a part of us that is drawn to vices. We know that if indulged, this part of us could take over our whole personality. However, God offers something to help us that is stronger than any serum: His Holy Spirit. Through God's Spirit, Christians can subdue the "Hyde" within and become more and more genuinely "Jekyll."

In this session, we will look at the powerful transforming grace of God. We will examine how we no longer need to be slaves of sin because, through Jesus, we can be set free to desire and pursue right living.

1. *Without naming names, what are some bad habits that you have witnessed Jesus break in other people through the power of His transforming grace?*

2. *What are some good qualities that you have seen in yourself or others that you credit to the influence of Jesus?*

EXPERIENCE IT

I am gracious and compassionate, slow to anger and rich in Love. Explore the wonders of grace: unmerited favor lavished on you through My finished work on the cross. *By grace you have been saved through faith, and that not of yourself; it is the gift of God.* What's more, *My compassions never fail. They are new every morning.* So begin your day expectantly, ready to receive fresh compassions. Don't let yesterday's failures weigh you down. Learn from your mistakes and confess known sins, but don't let those become your focus. Instead, keep your eyes on Me.

I am *slow to anger.* So don't be quick to judge yourself—or others. Rather, rejoice that I am *rich in Love.* In fact, Love is at the very core of who I am. Your growth in grace involves learning to be more attentive to Me, more receptive to My loving Presence. This requires vigilant effort because the evil one despises your closeness to Me. Strive to stay alert, and remember: *There is no condemnation for those who belong to Me!*

—FROM *JESUS ALWAYS,* SEPTEMBER 20

3. *Do you tend to let yesterday's failures weigh you down? What can help you not do this?*

_____

_____

_____

4. *Why does living a life of grace require vigilant effort if grace is received and not earned?*

_____

_____

_____

_____

Through My resurrection from the dead, you have *new birth into a living hope*. My work in you is all about "newness." Because you belong to Me, you're *a new creation; the old has gone, the new has come!* Your adoption into My royal family occurred instantaneously, at the moment you first trusted Me as Savior. At that instant, your spiritual status changed from death to life—eternal Life. You have *an inheritance that can never perish, spoil, or fade—kept in heaven for you*.

You are indeed a new creation, with the Holy Spirit living in you. But your becoming a Christian was only the *beginning* of the work I'm doing in you. You need *to be made new in the attitude of your mind and to put on the new self*—becoming increasingly godly, righteous, and holy. This is a lifelong endeavor, and it is preparing you for heaven's Glory. So receive this assignment with courage and gratitude. Be alert, and look for all the wonderful things I am doing in your life.

—FROM *JESUS ALWAYS*, MARCH 27

5. *If you are a Christian, how are you experiencing newness in your life with Jesus?*

_____

_____

_____

_____

6. *How would you like to experience newness in your life with Jesus? What would you like Him to transform?*

_____

_____

_____

_____

Study It

Read Romans 6:1–14. The apostle Paul taught that because believers are saved by grace, they are not obligated to live by the Jewish law laid out in the Old Testament. Some of his critics had charged that he was telling people it didn't matter how they lived, because there was grace to cover all their sins. So, in this passage, Paul explained why that was a serious misunderstanding of what he was saying. He says that those who live under grace rather than the law have a huge motivation to say no to sin. In fact, the life of grace is a transformed life of freedom from sin.

[1] What shall we say, then? Shall we go on sinning so that grace may increase? [2] By no means! We are those who have died to sin; how can we live in it any longer? [3] Or don't you know that all of us who were baptized into Christ Jesus were baptized into his death? [4] We were therefore buried with him through baptism into death in order that, just as Christ was raised from the dead through the glory of the Father, we too may live a new life.

[5] For if we have been united with him in a death like his, we will certainly also be united with him in a resurrection like his. [6] For we know that our old self was crucified with him so that the body ruled by sin might be done away with, that we should no longer be slaves to sin—[7] because anyone who has died has been set free from sin.

[8] Now if we died with Christ, we believe that we will also live with him. [9] For we know that since Christ was raised from the dead, he cannot die again; death no longer has mastery over him. [10] The death he died, he died to sin once for all; but the life he lives, he lives to God.

[11] In the same way, count yourselves dead to sin but alive to God in Christ Jesus. [12] Therefore do not let sin reign in your mortal body so that you obey its evil desires. [13] Do not offer any part of yourself to sin as an instrument of wickedness, but rather offer yourselves to God as those who have been brought from death to life; and offer every part of yourself to him as an instrument of righteousness. [14] For sin shall no longer be your master, because you are not under the law, but under grace.

7. *What does Paul mean when he says believers have "died to sin" (verse 2)?*

8. *Paul says we are no longer slaves to sin (see verse 6). This implies that those who don't follow Jesus are slaves to sin. In what sense are nonbelievers slaves to sin while believers are not?*

9. *If you are a Christian, how real is it to you that you have died with Jesus and come to life again a new person? What helps you keep that awareness as you go through your day?*

10. *What are some ways you can count yourself "dead to sin" when it comes to living the way God intends for you to live (see verse 11)?*

11. *Do you regularly offer every part of yourself to God as an instrument of righteousness (see verse 13)? If so, how do you do this?*

12. *Take two minutes of silence to reread the passage, looking for a sentence, phrase, or even one word that stands out as something Jesus may want you to focus on in your life. If you're meeting with a group, the leader will keep track of time. At the end of two minutes, you may share with the group the word or phrase that came to you in the silence.*

13. *Read the passage aloud again. Take another two minutes of silence, prayerfully considering what response God might want you to make to what you have read in His Word. If you're meeting with a group, the leader will again keep track of time. At the end of two minutes, you may share with the group what came to you in the silence if you wish.*

14. *If you're meeting with a group, how can the members pray for you? If you're using this study on your own, what would you like to say to God right now?*

LIVE IT

This week, the theme of each reading will focus on the transformation that grace makes possible in the lives of those who accept Christ as their Savior. Read each passage slowly, pausing to think about what is being said. Rather than approaching this as an assignment to complete, think of it as an opportunity to meet with the One who loves you most. Use any of the questions that are helpful.

Day 1

Read Ephesians 4:17–19. What stands out to you in this description of what life is like for those who don't believe in Jesus?

What form would hard-heartedness take in you if you chose that path?

If you are a Christian, how has being others-focused instead of self-focused affected your outlook on life?

_____

_____

_____

_____

Thank God today for His offer to liberate you from living a life based on yourself.

Day 2

Read Ephesians 4:20–24. If you are a Christian, what has putting off the old self required you to do? (You might remind yourself of the "old self" as described in verses 17–19.)

_____

_____

_____

_____

In what ways are the desires of the old self deceitful (see verse 22)? How can they deceive you?

_____

_____

_____

_____

What are some of the qualities of a believer's "new self" that aren't yet solid in you?

_____

_____

_____

Ask God to help you put on the "new self" in some concrete way today.

Day 3

Read Ephesians 4:25–28. What qualities of the old self does Paul single out for mention here? Why do you think they are so important to pay attention to?

_____

_____

_____

Do you struggle with any of these qualities? If so, which ones?

_____

_____

_____

How do you deal with anger so that you are admitting it but not sinning in it? What is a constructive way to deal with anger?

_____

_____

_____

_____

Be aware today of any inclination to deceit or anger. If something does make you angry (or even irritated), devise a way to deal with it that doesn't lead to sin.

Day 4

Read Ephesians 4:29–31. What are some kinds of unwholesome talk that would potentially come out of your mouth (see verse 29)?

_____

_____

_____

In what ways can you build others up with your speech?

_____

_____

_____

In the context of Paul's other comments here, what do you think it means to "grieve" the Holy Spirit (see verse 30)?

_____

_____

_____

Today, pay attention to what talk comes out of your mouth. Notice anything that doesn't build others up or that is bitter, and confess it to God.

Day 5

Read 2 Corinthians 3:17–18. How does a person contemplate or behold the Lord's glory? What does that mean in practice?

How does contemplating the Lord's glory lead to being transformed into His image? Why would it work that way?

How could you make more space in your life to contemplate the Lord's glory?

Take some time today to simply contemplate the Lord's glory.

WEAKNESS
AND GRACE

CONSIDER IT

Charles Haddon Spurgeon was arguably one of the greatest preachers of the nineteenth century. He became famous in London at the age of nineteen, preaching to thousands every week. But when he was twenty-one, God allowed him to experience a tragedy that made it impossible for him to be conceited about his achievement.

One night in a packed auditorium, some malcontents yelled, "Fire!" The panic that followed left seven people dead and many more injured. Spurgeon collapsed with anxiety, depression, and physical illness as a result of the event and couldn't preach for three weeks. This was the first of many bouts of depression and illness that would plague him throughout his life. His preaching was fabulously popular, but his critics were vicious and his ailments kept him bedridden for weeks—and sometimes months at a time.

In 1871 Spurgeon wrote, "It is a great mercy to be able to change sides when lying in bed . . . Did you ever lie a week on one side? Did you ever try to turn, and find yourself quite helpless?" He clearly knew how reliant he was on the Lord, and yet, by the time he died at the age of fifty-seven, he had published thousands of sermons and pastored huge churches for decades. It was possible only by the grace of God.

In this session, we will look at a passage from the apostle Paul that parallels Spurgeon's experience. We will see how often grace goes with weakness so that God gets all the glory.

1. *What is one of your weaknesses—not a sin, but an area where you suffer or are not gifted?*

_____

_____

_____

_____

2. *How do you usually deal with your weaknesses? Do you hide them? Ask God to take them away? Resent them? Explain.*

EXPERIENCE IT

When you begin a day—or a task—feeling inadequate, remember this: *My grace is sufficient for you.* The present tense of the verb "is" highlights the continual availability of My wondrous grace. So don't waste energy regretting how weak you feel. Instead, embrace your insufficiency— rejoicing that it helps you realize how much you need Me. Come to Me for help, and delight in My infinite sufficiency! *My Power is made perfect in weakness.*

As you go about a task in joyful dependence on Me, you will be surprised by how much you can accomplish. Moreover, the quality of your work will be greatly enhanced by your collaboration with Me. Ponder the astonishing privilege of living and working alongside Me, the *King of kings and Lord of lords.* Seek to align yourself with My will, making yourself a *living sacrifice.* This is a form of worship, and it pleases Me. It also makes your life meaningful and joyful. This is a tiny foretaste of the immense, indescribably glorious Joy that awaits you in heaven!

—FROM *JESUS ALWAYS*, MAY 16

3. *What would it look like to embrace your insufficiencies?*

4. *Have you ever been surprised at how much you could accomplish when aided by God? If so, describe the experience.*

Learn to lean on Me more and more. I know the full extent of your weakness, and that is where My powerful Presence meets you! My strength and your weakness fit together perfectly—in a wonderful synergy designed long before your birth. Actually, *My Power is most effective in weakness.* This is counterintuitive and mysterious, yet it is true.

It's important to lean on Me when you're feeling inadequate or overwhelmed. Remind yourself that you and I *together* are more than adequate. To sense my nearness, try closing your hand as if you're holding onto Mine. *For I take hold of your right hand and say to you, "Do not fear; I will help you."*

I want you to depend on Me even when you feel competent to handle things yourself. This requires awareness of both My Presence and your neediness. I am infinitely wise, so let Me guide your thinking as you make plans and decisions. Leaning on Me produces warm intimacy with Me—the One who *will never leave you or forsake you.*

—FROM *JESUS ALWAYS*, OCTOBER 12

5. *What helps you to remember to lean on God?*

6. *What are the things in the world that pull us away from leaning on God?*

_____

_____

_____

STUDY IT

Read 2 Corinthians 12:1–10. In this passage, Paul is defending his apostolic authority to the Corinthians, who have met some other apostles who seem more impressive than he is. They admire these other apostles for their preaching skill and forceful manner. In response, Paul—instead of boasting about his skills, his understanding of theology, or his gifts as a pastor—chooses instead to boast of the suffering he has undergone for the sake of the gospel. He has already talked about the hunger, prison, beatings, shipwrecks, and other hardships he has faced for Jesus' sake. Now he continues to boast in a way that he hopes will cure the Corinthians of being impressed with the wrong things. (Note that it is unknown what Paul was referring to when he mentioned his "thorn in the flesh.")

> [1] I must go on boasting. Although there is nothing to be gained, I will go on to visions and revelations from the Lord. [2] I know a man in Christ who fourteen years ago was caught up to the third heaven. Whether it was in the body or out of the body I do not know—God knows. [3] And I know that this man—whether in the body or apart from the body I do not know, but God knows—[4] was caught up to paradise and heard inexpressible things, things that no one is permitted to tell. [5] I will boast about a man like that, but I will not boast about myself, except about my weaknesses. [6] Even if I should choose to boast, I would not be a fool, because I would be speaking the truth. But I refrain, so no one will think more of me than is warranted by what I do or say, [7] or because of these surpassingly great revelations. Therefore, in order to keep me from becoming conceited, I was given a thorn in my flesh,

a messenger of Satan, to torment me. [8] Three times I pleaded with the Lord to take it away from me. [9] But he said to me, "My grace is sufficient for you, for my power is made perfect in weakness." Therefore I will boast all the more gladly about my weaknesses, so that Christ's power may rest on me. [10] That is why, for Christ's sake, I delight in weaknesses, in insults, in hardships, in persecutions, in difficulties. For when I am weak, then I am strong.

7. *The other apostles the Corinthians met boasted about their spiritual experiences, so Paul feels obliged to mention one of the visions and revelations he has experienced (see verses 1–4). This is the only place in the New Testament where Paul even mentions that he has had visions. As a leader, why would he be so reticent to share this?*

8. *Why does Paul boast about his weaknesses? Why does he feel they are important to his leadership qualifications?*

9. *What do people you know tend to look for in Christian leaders?*

10. *The Lord says to Paul, "My grace is sufficient for you" (verse 9). How would you explain in your own words what this means?*

11. *How can "thorns in the flesh" positively affect a Christian's ability to serve and share about Jesus with others? Give an example that you've witnessed.*

12. *Take two minutes of silence to reread the passage, looking for a sentence, phrase, or even one word that stands out as something Jesus may want you to focus on in your life. If you're meeting with a group, the leader will keep track of time. At the end of two minutes, you may share with the group the word or phrase that came to you in the silence.*

13. *Read the passage aloud again. Take another two minutes of silence, prayerfully considering what response God might want you to make to what you have read in His Word. If you're meeting with a group, the leader will* *again keep track of time. At the end of two minutes, you may share with the group what came to you in the silence if you wish.*

---

14. *If you're meeting with a group, how can the members pray for you? If you're using this study on your own, what would you like to say to God right now?*

LIVE IT

This week, the theme of each reading will focus on weakness and God's grace. Read each passage slowly, pausing to think about what is being said. Rather than approaching this as an assignment to complete, think of it as an opportunity to meet with the One who loves you most. Use any of the questions that are helpful.

Day 1

Read Romans 8:26–27. How does the Holy Spirit help believers in their weakness? With what weakness does this passage say the Holy Spirit helps?

Is this an area of weakness for you? If you are a believer, how does the Holy Spirit help you?

How do you respond to the Holy Spirit's help? Is this a shrug for you, or are you thankful? Do you tend to seek this help, or do you ignore it?

Today, thank the Holy Spirit for helping followers of Christ in prayer.

Day 2

Read 1 Corinthians 1:25–29. How is the weakness of God stronger than human strength?

To what degree does the description of people in verses 26–29 apply to you? How do you feel about this?

Why does God choose the weak over the strong? What does this say about Him?

_____

_____

_____

Today, think of some of the people in your life, and forgive their weaknesses.

Day 3

Read 1 Corinthians 2:1–5. How does it affect you to think of Paul doing his ministry with weakness, fear, and trembling (see verse 3)?

_____

_____

_____

Do you think there is ever a place for wise and persuasive words when it comes to spreading the gospel? Why did you answer the way you did?

_____

_____

_____

Paul was able to demonstrate the Holy Spirit's power. How do you think he did this? Would you be fearful if you were able to do that? Why or why not?

_____

_____

_____

If you feel fear today, remind yourself that Paul did as well, and go to God for your strength.

Day 4

Read 2 Corinthians 4:7–12. What does Paul mean when he describes himself as a jar of clay?

The treasure is the gospel and the presence of God. Why do you think it's so important to God that people know the power is from Him and not from themselves?

How does it affect you to think about Paul going through what he describes in verses 8–11? Can you identify with him to any degree?

Today, think about yourself as a clay jar full of treasure.

Day 5

Read Hebrews 4:14–16. How does it help you to know that Jesus is able to empathize with your weaknesses?

Why do you think this passage refers to God's throne as the "throne of grace"? What does this mean?

As a believer in Christ, how have you experienced God's throne as a throne of grace?

Spend some time today going to God's throne of grace to seek help for your time of need.

LEADER'S NOTES

Thank you for your willingness to lead a group through this *Jesus Always* study. The rewards of leading are different from the rewards of participating, and we hope you find your own walk with Jesus deepened by this experience. In many ways, your group meeting will be structured like other Bible studies in which you've participated. You'll want to open in prayer, for example, and ask people to silence their phones. These leader's notes will focus on elements of the study that may be new to you.

CONSIDER IT

This first portion of the study functions as an icebreaker. It gets the group members thinking about the topic at hand by asking them to share from their own experience. Some people may be tempted to tell a long story in response to one of these questions, but the goal is to keep the answers brief. Ideally, you want everyone in the group to have a chance to answer the *Consider It* questions, so you may want to say up front that everyone needs to limit his or her answer to one minute.

With the rest of the study, it is generally not a good idea to go around the circle and have everyone answer every question—a free-flowing discussion is more desirable. But with the *Consider It* questions, you can go around the circle. Encourage shy people to share, but don't force them. Tell the group they should feel free to pass if they prefer not to answer a question.

EXPERIENCE IT

This is the group's chance to talk about excerpts from the *Jesus Always* devotional. You will need to monitor this discussion closely so that you have enough time for the actual study of God's Word that follows. If the group has a long and rich discussion on one of the devotional excerpts, you may choose to skip the other one and move on to the Bible study. Don't feel obliged to cover every *Experience It* question if the conversation is fruitful. On the other hand, do move on if the group gets off on a tangent.

STUDY IT

Try to do the *Study It* exercise in session 1 on your own before the group meets the first time so you can coach people on what to expect. Note that this section may be a little different from Bible studies your group has done in the past. The group will talk about the Bible passage as usual, but then there will be several minutes of silence so individuals can pray about what God might want to say to them personally through the reading. It will be up to you to keep track of the time and call people back to the discussion when the time is up. (There are some good timer apps that play a gentle chime or other pleasant sound instead of a disruptive noise.) If members aren't used to being silent in a group, brief them on what to expect.

Don't be afraid to let people sit in silence. Two minutes of quiet may seem like a long time at first, but it will help to train group members to sit in silence with God when they are alone. They can remain where they are in the circle, or if you have space, you can let them go off by themselves to other rooms at your instruction. If your group meets in a home, ask the host before the meeting which rooms are available for use. Some people will be more comfortable in the quiet if they have a bit of space from others.

When the group reconvenes after the time of silence, invite them to share what they experienced. There are several questions provided in this study guide that you can ask. Note that it's not necessary to cover every question if the group has a good discussion going. It's also not necessary to go around the circle and make everyone share.

Don't be concerned if the group members are reserved and slow to share after the exercise. People are often quiet when they are pulling together their ideas, and the exercise will have been a new experience for many of them. Just ask a question and let it hang in the air until someone speaks up. You can then say, "Thank you. What about others? What came to you when you sat with the passage?"

Some people may say they found it hard to quiet their minds enough to focus on the passage for those few minutes. Tell them this is okay. They are practicing a skill, and sometimes skills take time to learn. If they learn to sit quietly with God's Word in a group, they will become much more comfortable sitting with the Word on their own. Remind them that spending time in the Bible each day is one of the most valuable things they can do as believers in Christ.

Preparation

It's not necessary for group members to prepare anything for the study ahead of time. However, at the end of each study are five days' worth of suggestions for spending time in God's Word during the next week. These daily times are optional but valuable, so encourage the group to do them. Also, invite them to bring their questions and insights to the group at your next meeting, especially if they had a breakthrough moment or if they didn't understand something.

As the leader, there are a few things you should do to prepare for each meeting:

- *Read through the session.* This will help you become familiar with the content and know how to structure the discussion times.

- *Spend five to ten minutes doing the* Study It *questions on your own.* When the group meets, you'll be watching the clock, so you'll probably have a more fulfilling time with the passage if you do the exercise ahead of time. You can then spend time in the passage again with the group. This way, you'll be sure to have the key verses for that session deeply in your mind.

- *Pray for your group.* Pray especially that God will guide them in how to embrace the love that Jesus has demonstrated for them and, in turn, share that love with others in their world who need to experience it.

- *Bring extra supplies to your meeting.* Group members should bring their own pens for writing notes on the Bible reflection, but it is a good idea to have extras available for those who forget. You may also want to bring paper and Bibles for those who may have neglected to bring their study guides to the meeting.

Below you will find suggested answers for some of the study questions. Note that in many cases there is no one right answer, especially when the group members are sharing their personal experiences.

Session 1: Unearned Grace

1. *Answers will vary. The goal here is for the group members to get to know each other better and to become aware that while we sometimes respond to grace with gratitude, at other times we can be confused and unnerved by it.*

2. *Answers will vary. Having no rules as a child, or failing to have consequences for broken rules, is not the same as grace. Grace-filled parents have rules and fair consequences, but they sometimes pay the consequences themselves when they discern this is best in the moment. However, if parents always pay the consequences, children won't learn to become responsible adults, especially as they get older. But if children grow up being held accountable for their actions while also being treated with love and respect, a moment of grace can speak volumes.*

3. *The very fact that we're alive is evidence of God's unearned favor, as is God's desire for relationship with His creation, and (for many) the physical and mental capacity to work for a living. We have been given so much that we didn't earn. Furthermore, God's offer to forgive our sins, which we can't see but can know by faith, is one of the biggest unearned favors we have.*

4. *Answers will vary. The group members can take a look at their own lives to see how they respond each day. The truth is that many of us tend to take God's favor for granted and are inclined to grumble that we don't have more. However, it's important for us to notice all the good things that God sends into our lives each day and respond with gratitude.*

5. *Some of us try to work hard to "earn" God's love, even though He has said in His Word that His children can't earn it—it's freely given and already ours (see Ephesians 2:8–9). Others of us tend to approach grace with an attitude of* entitlement. *Although truly humble people are often unaware they're humble (they don't think about themselves much), each of us can at least notice if we're off on one of these two wrong tracks when it comes to grace.*

6. *As God's children, knowing that we cannot lose His love should empower us to live unencumbered and without constantly striving to please anyone other than Him. It should lift shame and guilt from our shoulders. It should also make us more generous and gracious toward other people.*

7. *The laborers who were hired first received what they deserved. Note that the landowner's offer to this first group was entirely fair. Day workers at the time who were not hired first thing in the morning stayed in the marketplace, hoping for work, because their families typically only had food when they could find work. Those hired later in the day all received more than they deserved, especially those who the landowner hired last.*

8. *The laborers who were hired first were upset because they were comparing the work and payment they received to the work and payment the laborers who came after them received. It didn't seem fair to them, but then the landowner reminded them that they had received what had been promised to them. In the same way, we can often be angered by grace that we see given to someone else. If we have been treated fairly, we don't have rational grounds to be angry, but somehow, when someone else is treated more than fairly, it often feels unfair.*

9. *Jesus' parable points to the fact that all believers in Christ, no matter how long or how hard they have worked during this lifetime, will receive the same basic reward: eternal life. However, heaven's value system is different from the one on earth, and those who are not held in high regard on this earth may be held in high esteem in heaven. Jesus was pointing to the fact that we can't get caught up in the world's way of ranking things, but must look to God's way.*

10. *Answers will vary. Some group members may have been believers in Christ since childhood and faithfully serving God all that time. Some may have become believers as adults. Some may be new believers. God loves all* *these groups and considers them equal heirs of His kingdom. Therefore, those who have been serving for a long time need to avoid looking down on those who enter the kingdom late in life.*

11. *Envy becomes a temptation when we put the highest value on the material things of this world, such as money, physical beauty, or status. If these things are more valuable to us than what God offers to us for free—such as His love, mercy, and grace—then we will live in competition with others to have the most material goods.*

12. *Answers will vary. It's fine for this process to be unfamiliar to the group at first. Be sure to keep track of time.*

13. *Answers will vary. Note that some people may find the silence intimidating at first. Their anxiety might tempt them to fill the air with noise, but it will be helpful for these group members to just take a quiet moment before God. Let them express their discomfort once you're all gathered together again, but make sure it is balanced by those who found the silence strengthening. Helping people become comfortable with this "holy quiet" will serve their private daily times with God in wonderful ways.*

14. *Take as much time as you can to pray for each other. You might have someone write down the prayer requests so you can keep track of answers to prayer.*

Session 2: Outrageous Grace

1. *The story of the traffic accident is outrageous because we naturally believe that justice should prevail in society. Actions should have consequences, and people who do wrong things should have to pay the price. After all, if other people were constantly rescuing them from themselves, they would never learn to grow up and take responsibility. God is a God of justice, and He has set up a world where actions do have consequences. Yet in a situation where actions have devastating consequences—eternal death—He offers to intervene on our behalf to rescue us. We're meant to feel the incomprehensibility of this action on His part.*

2. *Answers will vary. It's good for the group members to develop the habit of noticing when God enriches their lives with a moment of beauty or goodness out of the blue. This can help them cultivate gratitude. Those small moments are evidence of God's presence in this world.*

3. *There are many ways Christians can be affected if we carry around unnecessary guilt. We can act withdrawn, or we can be quick to blame other people when they do something wrong, or we can work hard to be perfect to compensate for our feelings of guilt and shame. By contrast, if we have accepted God's gift of grace and are truly aware that we have been forgiven for our sins, we are more likely to be especially compassionate and merciful toward other sinners, and we are more likely to reach out in love toward others.*

4. *If followers of Christ are not finding meaning in their identity as children of God, it is likely because they are working hard to find meaning in something else. For example, we may find ourselves living vicariously through our children, finding our primary identity as their parents, and putting extra pressure on them as a result. Or we may find meaning in our work and tend to work too hard.*

5. *One thing we can do as followers of Christ is to have set times of the day when we cycle around and revisit this truth so it never gets stale. We can develop a habit of rehearsing this truth when we get up in the morning, before each meal, and before we go to bed at night. We can continually say to ourselves, "I'm a member of a royal family. What difference does that make in my life at this present moment?"*

6. *As followers of Christ, we can help others see Jesus as the source of life by showing compassion for them and taking a genuine interest in their lives. If those people are ever curious about what drives us, we can talk about Jesus and the difference He has made in our lives. We can make a point of extending ourselves in sacrificial love toward others, doing whatever we can to serve them, and doing it joyfully. We can talk about how thankful we are for life and monitor our speech so that it reflects an attitude of abundance rather than scarcity.*

7. *The first outrageous thing the father does is to not just slap his younger son and tell him to show respect when the boy asks for his share of the estate. Instead, the father divides his estate (most of it would be in land, which would require selling it to come up with cash) and gives his ungrateful son the money. Then, months or years after the rebellious son leaves home, the father watches for him in case he returns home (see verse 20). When the father sees his son coming, he then casts aside his dignity, runs to his son, and kisses him. He gives him all the marks of sonship and authority, including a robe, ring, and sandals (see verse 22). The father orders the calf reserved for special occasions to be killed, and then throws a party. He does all of these acts for a young man who deserves to be rejected. The father doesn't make his son pay any negative consequences for his actions beyond what he experienced in the distant country.*

8. *Answers will vary. Some group members may have been faithful Christians from their youth, but most will identify with the younger son in at least one period of their lives.*

9. *Responses will vary. It can be easy for any of us to get into a mindset where we are counting our disappointments instead of our blessings. Even longtime Christians can feel jealous at times that God doesn't seem to throw parties for them—but instead welcomes "low-lifes" into the kingdom. Like the older brother, the sons and daughters of God may sometimes question our Father's love and lack overflowing gratitude that He is constantly with us.*

10. *Each of us are called to be like the father in the story, extending grace to the undeserving (though it's certainly much easier to receive grace than to give it). We can give grace more effectively if we will reflect on God's overwhelming graciousness toward us. This will more quickly enable us to stop demanding that people should be treated the way they deserve. Sometimes "tough love" is necessary to help another person, but other situations call for grace. The Holy Spirit can help believers discern which of these is appropriate in any given moment, if they will look to Him.*

11. *God doesn't give grace to those who feel entitled to it. The older son felt entitled, and it was ruining his relationship with his father. Repentance and humility are key. We can't say for sure what would have happened if the younger son had sauntered home and continued to treat his father with disrespect, but a true reconciliation would have been impossible in that case.*

12. *Answers will vary.*

13. *Answers will vary.*

14. *Responses will vary.*

Session 3: Rescuing Grace

1. *God is holy, and He wants us to have high moral standards that allow us to live in such a way that we will bring honor to Him. He loves justice and goodness, and He longs to weave them into our lives. He wants us to live the way Jesus would live if He were in our shoes. Having high moral standards takes all of that seriously and makes it possible for us to increasingly act like Jesus.*

2. *High moral standards can quickly degenerate into legalism if we don't balance them with the grace of forgiveness and offer people second chances. In addition, if we know we're not living up to these high standards, we can end up hiding and pretending, which doesn't honor God and only leaves us in isolation and anger or fear. These problems can be avoided simply by adding grace to the high standards. Both children and adults need to be taught that they can confess their wrongdoing and be forgiven. Confession needs to be met without shaming and with the goal of restoring the relationship, even if consequences have to be paid.*

3. *Answers will vary. The group members may mention the world sends messages of such conditional love and acceptance through the influence of television programs, movies, or social media, or through past dating* experiences, or through situations they've had in childhood with parents, teachers, religious authorities, and classmates in school.

4. *Spending time in prayer and reading God's Word is essential to helping God's children know that they can approach the throne of grace for forgiveness. The Bible includes many real-life examples of people of faith who sinned and received the Lord's pardon after repenting. These stories can be a great encouragement to us. It's also helpful if we have people in our lives who practice grace with us and with others. Ideally, we each have at least one person with whom we can be honest about our mistakes.*

5. *Answers will vary. Some of the group members may have difficulty seeing themselves in God's eyes if the key figures in their lives (such as their parents or their close friends growing up) didn't treat them with grace. However, this can change for followers of Christ over time as we soak in God's presence and reflect on what His Word says about us.*

6. *Answers will vary. Again, it is easy even for followers of Christ to project onto God the bad experiences they have had with other people. If the key people in our lives are not grace-filled, we can easily feel condemned when God's gentle murmur points out an area of our behavior that needs to improve. We need to practice distinguishing His voice from the voices of the graceless people who surround us in our lives.*

7. *To the Pharisees and teachers of the law, the woman is just a pawn in their schemes against Christ. They don't even consider her to be a person. They have the setup they want, and now they are publicly shaming her—all in order to get at Jesus. They are entirely willing to kill her in their quest to bring Jesus down.*

8. *Jesus waits until He is alone with the woman to speak to her. He addresses her as "woman," which was a term of respect that He used even with His mother (see John 2:4). He doesn't ask her to defend herself—they both know she is guilty. Instead, He graciously frees her from the lawful consequences of* her act. He doesn't minimize her sin but tells her not to do it again, and He's aware that this whole experience and her encounter with Him will motivate her not to repeat her wrong behavior.

9. *Jesus is more interested in repentance and changed lives than He is with punishment. He judges that in this situation, asking the woman to pay more consequences for her sin is unnecessary. The humiliation and near death at the hands of the religious leaders has been punishment enough, and a forgiving encounter with Him will transform her for the future. Also, Jesus has the right to pardon sin, because He is going to pay the price for it.*

10. *Answers will vary. For example, the church shouldn't minimize adultery, because it's a serious sin. The goal should be getting the parties to stop the sin, admit that they've done wrong, and take steps toward an amended life. Restitution should be made to the harmed spouses. "Go now and leave your life of sin" is a good guideline. People who are unwilling to stop the adultery should be disciplined. This is hard but necessary.*

11. *Condemnation is about punishment and judgment. However, accountability aims at changing the person's life for the better. Condemnation wouldn't have given the woman in this story another chance to do life better. Jesus wasn't overlooking the consequences of her actions, but He knew that this was a time for grace.*

12. *Answers will vary.*

13. *Answers will vary.*

14. *Responses will vary.*

Session 4: Sacrificing Grace

1. *In Leviticus 17:11, God said to His people, "For the life of a creature is in the blood, and I have given it to you to make atonement for yourselves on the altar; it is the blood that makes atonement for one's life." We live in a* *culture in which animal sacrifice is no longer practiced by major religions, so we can easily forget that this was prevalent in both Old Testament and New Testament times. The culture of Jesus' time understood that blood was required to be shed to satisfy God's justice and set people free from their sins.*

2. *Answers will vary. You will likely not have enough time for the group members to share their testimonies in detail. However, this is a good chance for you to get to know whether they were children or adults when they first encountered the gospel and how they responded to the idea of Jesus dying on the cross for their sins.*

3. *As we read in 1 John 1:9, followers of Christ don't need to be afraid to face their sins because they know that Jesus has already secured the Father's forgiveness for them. God has clothed His children in His own righteousness (see Isaiah 61:10) and His own moral perfection (see Hebrews 10:14) so that they may be in right standing with Him (see 2 Corinthians 5:18). Our sinning doesn't shock God, and it doesn't mean we're worthless. We simply need to confess our sins and thank Him for clothing us in His righteousness.*

4. *As followers of Christ, we don't need to dwell on past failures and past sin that we have already confessed because those past mistakes don't define us. Self-loathing is a poison, and we don't have to drink it, because Jesus' sacrifice means that all our faults are forgiven. We can simply confess our sins and ask for God's strength to do better.*

5. *Even a great truth like the forgiveness of sins can become something followers of Christ take for granted. But that's a tragedy! Forgiveness is something for which believers need to be thankful on a daily basis. If we come to grips with the fact that we've perhaps lost the thrill of forgiveness, it can help to spur us back to this awareness with fresh joy.*

6. *There are many benefits of practicing gratitude for forgiveness. For example, it will help us avoid sin—it makes sin less attractive. Also, it will help us avoid both pride and self-loathing.*

7. *Jesus offered His life for those who follow Him as a gift, completely unearned. His death rescued them from slavery to sin, death, and Satan, setting them free to be His brothers and sisters in God's family. We could never have freed ourselves without His intervention.*

8. *Sinners acquire righteousness—a right relationship with God—through faith in Jesus. Faith isn't a meritorious thing we do to earn our place in God's family. Rather, it is a response of trust and gratitude to the gift of forgiveness that God is freely offering.*

9. *God's justice requires that sin have consequences. It can't just be swept under the carpet and ignored. Our rebellion against God honestly deserves the death penalty, and the harm we do to other people also deserves consequences. God doesn't want to kill the entire human race—He loves us so much that He made a way to deliver us from our sin. However, His justice requires that someone pay the penalty. So, Jesus died instead of us. All of God's justice poured the penalty of our sin on to the Son of God.*

10. *Answers will vary. Some examples may include that having a right relationship with God means we are free to approach Him in prayer at any time throughout the day. It means we will do our best to avoid sin, that we are free to acknowledge our sins to Him, and that we can be assured we will receive forgiveness. It means that God will guide us along the path He wants for our lives. We are His emissary into other people's lives.*

11. *Answers will vary. Not only does accepting Jesus' gift of redemption make us aware of our sins against God so that we are less prone to commit them in this life, but we don't have to be afraid of death because we know we will go to be with Jesus. We look forward to our own resurrection, when we will receive a new body in which we will live forever. Christ's redemption removes the fear of sin and death.*

12. *Answers will vary.*

13. *Answers will vary.*

14. *Responses will vary.*

Session 5: Glorious Grace

1. *Answers will vary. We need to practice paying attention so we can notice the large or small gestures of unearned favor that God grants to us each day, such as getting to see a beautiful sunset or connect heart-to-heart with another person. For believers, this might include recognizing the truth anew that we are forgiven.*

2. *Answers will vary. The main ways for us to respond to God's grace are through thankfulness and passing on the grace to someone else—treating someone else better than they deserve. Christians are people who love because they have been loved (see 1 John 4:19).*

3. *When we recognize that God approves of us, there's no room for feelings of insecurity, nor do we feel the need to strive for others' approval. As God's children, we have all the approval we need, lavished on us by our heavenly Father. For us, this means that instead of focusing on what we can achieve, we focus on loving others.*

4. *It can be hard for us to accept God's affirmation, even if we are Christians, because we internalize the messages of non-affirmation we receive from people in the world—and then we project those messages onto God. Also, we can't see or audibly hear God, so we don't pick up the face-to-face cues that would tell us He affirms us. And, in the Bible, we read about Him disciplining people for sin and assume that means He's generally angry. But He isn't. He delights in His children.*

5. *When the Bible says that "God is light" (1 John 1:5), it is referring to a spiritual form of light—God is righteous, pure, and completely holy. Each of God's sons and daughters has been called out of the darkness of sin and death to step into the light of eternal life with God. That is the spiritual geography of those who have put their faith in Christ: in the light, not the darkness. The* more God's people choose to live that way, the more they can see the right path forward. Soaking in God's light nurtures strength and peace.

6. As followers of Christ, we never reach a point where it's time to start "earning" our way into God's light. We will never deserve it—and that's okay. We will always need to be caught up in gratitude for what God is doing for us. And if ever we choose darkness for a period of time, we need to turn back to Him, change our ways, and be received back into fellowship with Him.

7. There are many benefits of being "in Christ." For example, we are considered holy and blameless in God's eyes. We are adopted as His adult children and heirs. We are given His glorious grace. We are redeemed by Jesus' blood—it buys us out of slavery to sin, death, and Satan. Our sins are forgiven. We come to know that God desires to bring all things into unity under Jesus Christ as ruler.

8. If we are children of God, knowing that we are holy and blameless in God's eyes should keep us from piling guilt and shame on ourselves. It should make us relax and enjoy Jesus' presence without pressure. It should make us joyfully committed to acting in a holy and blameless manner—and when we fail, we should be able to pick ourselves up again in the Lord's strength, confess our failure, and begin again.

9. If we have accepted God's offer to be His spiritual heirs, it should affect us by making us overflow with joy and gratitude for all of these blessings! Our spiritual adoption should take away any feelings of deprivation or scarcity that we have. We know that we are heirs of the universe and will one day share ownership of everything that God possesses. We don't have to be ashamed of being ordinary, because we're part of a royal family. We belong. Insecurity should be so far from our minds that we have far greater capacity to care for others.

10. Here again, all these blessings come to God's children as gifts, not as things they've earned through good behavior. We deserve God's anger because *of our rebelliousness, but instead of venting His well-earned anger on us, or just ignoring us, He determines to lavish these gifts of grace on us. This much grace is truly glorious.*

11. *One day, the order that was established at creation before the Fall will be re-established by God for His people. As Isaiah writes, "The wolf will live with the lamb" (11:6), and our earth will no longer be in rebellion against the Ruler who governs the universe. As John wrote, "[God] will wipe every tear from their eyes. There will be no more death or mourning or crying or pain, for the old order of things has passed away" (Revelation 21:4).*

12. *Answers will vary.*

13. *Answers will vary.*

14. *Responses will vary.*

Session 6: Saving Grace

1. *Answers will vary. Note that this question is meant to prepare the group members to study a passage of Scripture that contrasts life with God and life without Him in the starkest terms. Followers of Christ sometimes have trouble believing the contrast is that stark, because we see around us so many basically decent unbelievers who contribute good things to the world. It's hard to think that while we can celebrate the goodness of what they contribute, we should also lament that their lives are going to end in futility. Death will take everything from them.*

2. *Christians need not fear death because they know they will live on eternally. Our works of love, beauty, and goodness in this life have eternal significance, so we need not feel they are meaningless. Of course, death is not to be desired—it is the result of the fall, and we naturally try to avoid it and grieve when others are lost to it. This life is precious in God's eyes, so we should not do things that will hasten our death except as a sacrifice on behalf of others. However, Christians know that death is a time of temporary goodbyes—sad, but not permanent.*

3. *It's important to remind ourselves that salvation is a free gift of God because the world operates on the principle of earning—not of giving and receiving. The world tells us that we have to work to be good enough to be accepted by others. Our fallen minds and hearts have that bent as well, so they readily accept the world's attitude. And the devil chimes in with his accusations, telling us how far short of good enough we have fallen.*

4. *Some followers of Christ are just naturally shyer than others, which make them more reluctant to share what Jesus has done. Some of us fear rejection—the people around us seem perfectly happy and self-sufficient, so why would they listen to us? Whatever is holding us back, we need to pray for confidence in sharing the message of Christ and seeing others as God sees them—as people who are lost and in need of His grace. We need to approach them with respect and compassion, letting our thankfulness to God naturally overflow into care for them.*

5. *When we say that Jesus is "full of grace," it means He is full of an inclination to show unearned favor to those around Him. Grace is what people experience when they encounter Christ. The apostle John, who wrote that Jesus is full of grace (see John 1:14), went on to say that "from the fullness of his grace we have all received one blessing after another" (John 1:16). Jesus' grace overflows from within Him to fill those who receive Him with the blessings of salvation.*

6. *Answers will vary, but most of us dread failure or performing below the expectations we have set for ourselves. This dread can affect us in a variety of ways. On the one hand, it may make us driven to succeed and achieve. We may become excessively driven at work and neglect our relationships. Or we may drive our children to succeed, because in a way it feels as if their success represents our success as a parent. On the other hand, the fear of failure may paralyze us, making it hard for us to try anything difficult.*

7. *For some believers that time might have not been that long ago, so it is easy to remember their past lives. Others who came to faith in Jesus as children will likely not remember much of their past lives before Christ. Invite the group* members who have accepted Christ to recall when they followed the ways of this world. If the ways of this world continue to be alluring (as they are for many of us), they can talk about the things about the world system that attracts them.

8. *The flesh desires to be the center of attention. It craves possessions. It craves status. It craves power or control. Sometimes this is control over others, but if not, at least control over our own lives so we can do what we want when we want.*

9. *To be saved by grace means that a person has been rescued from eternal death and the futility of this life. As we have discussed, this offer of salvation comes to us completely as an unearned gift from God. Apart from Christ, we are objects of wrath—and we can do nothing to change the fact that we deserve the wrath of God.*

10. *God offers the gift of salvation, but it is a person's responsibility to respond in gratitude to that offer and accept it. Faith is the method by which we do this. Note again that having faith doesn't mean we've earned salvation—it simply means we choose to receive it. Faith says yes to the sacrifice of Jesus on our behalf and yes to the life that God wants us to lead. An important aspect of faith is that it includes giving the control to Jesus and trusting Him to run our lives.*

11. *As children of God, we are not saved by our good works, but are saved for good works. God has planned good things for His people to do to contribute to the world, and He calls us to do them. The works that we as Christians perform for others do not earn our salvation, but they represent a loving response on our part to the gift that God has extended to us.*

12. *Answers will vary.*

13. *Answers will vary.*

14. *Responses will vary.*

Session 7: Transforming Grace

1. *Answers will vary. As the group leader, make sure to direct the discussion away from the actual bad habits after they are mentioned and on to the power of Jesus' grace. Invite the group to consider habits that might not readily come to mind, such as self-absorption, pride, unbridled ambition, a harsh temper, or even hurtful gossip.*

2. *Answers will vary. For some believers, it's difficult to talk about the good qualities that they see in their lives. But it isn't prideful to be aware of good qualities that are attributable to God's work in our hearts. Think of the fruit of the Spirit: love, joy, peace, patience, goodness, kindness, faithfulness, gentleness, self-control. Do we have a measure of any of these?*

3. *If we are Christians, reminding ourselves that we have been saved by grace is a big help. We can remind ourselves each time a failure comes to mind. We can confess known sin and then let it go. It can be helpful to post verses from God's Word in places where we will see them each day, to assure us that we are completely forgiven for yesterday's failures. Playing praise and worship music with themes of forgiveness can also keep us focused on the truth at work, around the house, and as we run errands.*

4. *Living a life of grace does not involve "earning," but it does involve "effort." In fact, grace empowers effort in the life of a Christian. The New Testament is full of passages like the one the group will study today that provide believers with something they need to do in order to live in a way consistent with the grace that they have been extended. The effort is a response to the gift, as empowered by the gift.*

5. *Answers will vary. For some of the group members who are Christians, perhaps this takes the form of changing an attitude or a habit. Maybe they've learned something new about God. Other group members may have a hard time seeing anything new going on in their lives. They should feel free to say* *so. There are dry periods in every Christian's life—and maybe that's the new thing that's going on: learning to be faithful in the dry periods.*

6*. Answers will vary. This is a chance for the group members to dream big. What are they willing to ask God to do in their lives?*

7*. When Paul says that believers in Christ have "died to sin," he doesn't mean they are no longer tempted to sin or are unable to sin. Rather, Paul means that when we put our faith in Jesus, the change in our relationship to sin is as radical as a shift from life to death. We have figuratively drowned in the water of baptism and have emerged from the water with a resurrected life. It used to be impossible for us to say no to sin—but now it is possible for us to do so.*

8*. People who don't believe in Jesus can lead very good lives. And people who profess faith in Jesus can have some bad habits. The difference is that without Jesus, people are slaves to their determination to live on their own terms. Whatever bad habits they have are firmly rooted. But faith in Jesus introduces us to transforming grace, which makes it possible for us to uproot our bad habits. We find it possible to say no to those temptations.*

9*. Answers will vary. One of the reasons why it is important for believers to soak their minds in the Scriptures every day is to remind themselves of their death and rebirth in Christ. The world distracts us from truths like this and tells us we are stuck with our bad habits. But basking in Jesus' presence each day can reinforce the truth that we have died to all that is selfish and meaningless in us and that we have come back to life with vigor to serve God joyfully.*

10*. We can count ourselves dead to sin by accepting God's gift of forgiveness, looking at our bad habits, and saying, "I no longer have to be that way. I have the Holy Spirit helping me to live differently. I am under grace. I am dead to this sin and alive to God." Instead of depending on our own strength to say no, we can cry out to the Holy Spirit to empower us to say no. Every time the temptation comes back, we say, "I'm dead to that. I don't have to do that."*

11. *As Paul notes, believers in Christ are called to offer every part of themselves to God as an instrument of righteousness. We can do this by simply stating a prayer such as, "Lord, I offer You my tongue as an instrument of righteousness. Show me what to say today, and prompt me when to be silent. I offer You my hands as instruments of righteousness," and so on. Then we're on the alert during the day for chances to use our tongue or our hands to serve God.*

12. *Answers will vary.*

13. *Answers will vary.*

14. *Responses will vary.*

Session 8: Weakness and Grace

1. *Answers will vary. If the group members are shy about sharing their weaknesses, you can lead with one of your own to make them feel more at ease. The goal is not to highlight their area of weakness, but just to get them thinking about the idea of God's grace in the midst of it.*

2. *Answers will vary. There is no one right way to deal with a weakness. As we will see in the Bible passage for this week's study, Paul asked God to take a certain weakness away several times until God told him to live with it.*

3. *Embracing our insufficiencies might take the form of not avoiding a task we have to do because we think that we don't have the necessary abilities to do it. We simply ask God for the strength, and then we do our best at the task. And whether we succeed or fail, we rejoice that this experience can remind us of how much we need Jesus' strength in all things.*

4. *Answers will vary, but most followers of Christ have found themselves surprised at one time or another of something they could accomplish with God's strength that they never thought possible. If the group members have trouble coming up with examples, be sure to have a few examples of your own that you can offer.*

5. *Answers will vary. For followers of Christ, the experience of trying and failing at something can remind us to lean on God next time. Watching someone else leaning on God can also be helpful. For this reason, it's good if more mature believers are open about their weaknesses and need for God's strength, rather than trying to make everything look effortless.*

6. *There are many things in this world that can pull us away from leaning on God. For example, pride can pull us away, as can messages from the world about the need to always be self-reliant. "Believe in yourself" is the kind of message from the world that sounds good but will ultimately pull us away from putting our trust in God's grace.*

7. *Spiritual visions may build up the person who has them, but in most cases they do little for others who just hear about them. Paul never tried to "impress" his listeners with stories about how he had received visions to try to convince them of his leadership qualities. In the same way, when we evaluate our leaders, we shouldn't be persuaded by stories of their spiritual exploits but by the concrete things they have said and done.*

8. *Paul's weaknesses enable others to know that his ministry depends on God's power and not his own personality and gifts. Whatever Paul has accomplished has been God accomplishing it through him—so the right person gets the credit.*

9. *Answers will vary, but chances are high that most people look for strengths in their leaders, not for weaknesses. However, leaders who are humbly conscious of their weaknesses can be better leaders than those who are not. Weaknesses in this context aren't the same as sins.*

10. *This statement is less about God's forgiving grace and more about His empowering grace. This power of Paul's isn't his to claim but is the Lord working through him. When Paul writes letters, it is the Lord who gives him the wisdom regarding what to say. When he talks to people about Jesus, he* relies on the Lord rather than his own cleverness to know what to say. God's unearned strength is sufficient for Paul to get done what he needs to get done.

11. *Answers will vary. Some group members may feel that the things that weaken people (such as physical disabilities) can make it more difficult for people to serve others. However, Paul indicates that these things can actually make people more effective in others' lives as they see them rise above those weaknesses and continue to love others and trust God for strength.*

12. *Answers will vary.*

13. *Answers will vary.*

14. *Responses will vary.*

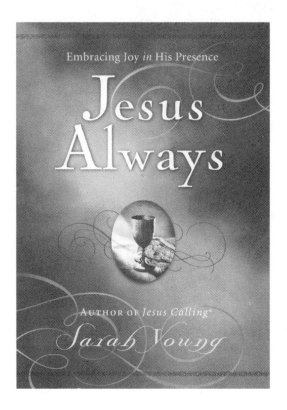

Also available in the
JESUS ALWAYS® BIBLE STUDY SERIES

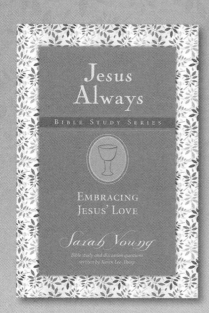

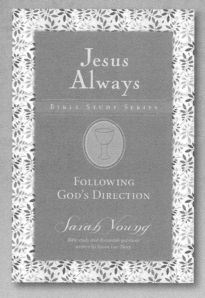

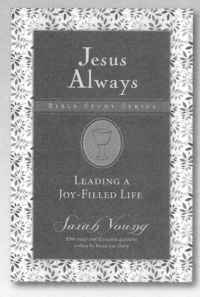

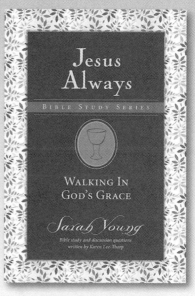

Also Available in the
Jesus Calling® Bible Study Series

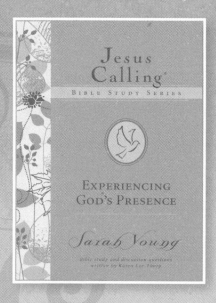

EXPERIENCING GOD'S PRESENCE

Sarah Young

Bible study and discussion questions
written by Karen Lee-Thorp

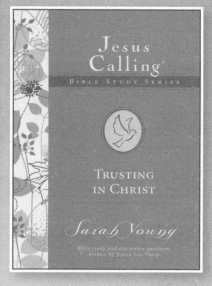

TRUSTING IN CHRIST

Sarah Young

Bible study and discussion questions
written by Karen Lee-Thorp

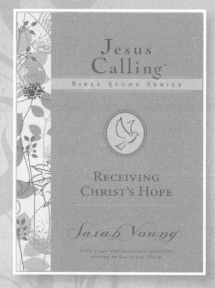

RECEIVING CHRIST'S HOPE

Sarah Young

Bible study and discussion questions
written by Karen Lee-Thorp

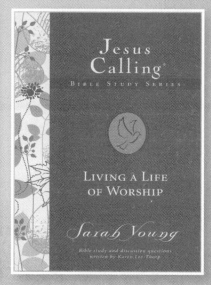

LIVING A LIFE OF WORSHIP

Sarah Young

Bible study and discussion questions
written by Karen Lee-Thorp

Also Available in the
Jesus Calling® Bible Study Series

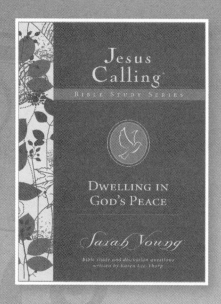

Jesus Calling
BIBLE STUDY SERIES

DWELLING IN
GOD'S PEACE

Sarah Young

Bible study and discussion questions
written by Karen Lee-Thorp

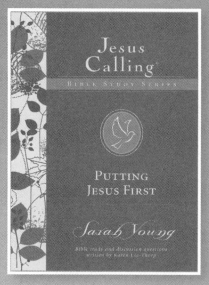

Jesus Calling
BIBLE STUDY SERIES

PUTTING
JESUS FIRST

Sarah Young

Bible study and discussion questions
written by Karen Lee-Thorp

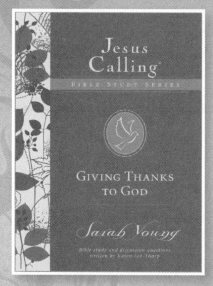

Jesus Calling
BIBLE STUDY SERIES

GIVING THANKS
TO GOD

Sarah Young

Bible study and discussion questions
written by Karen Lee-Thorp

Jesus Calling
BIBLE STUDY SERIES

LIVING WITH
GOD'S COURAGE

Sarah Young

Bible study and discussion questions
written by Karen Lee-Thorp

If you liked reading this book, you may enjoy
these other titles by *Sarah Young*

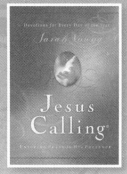

Jesus Calling®
Hardcover

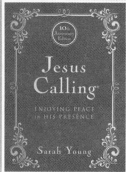

**Jesus Calling® 10th
Anniversary Edition**
Bonded Leather

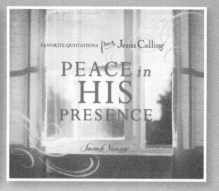

Peace in His Presence:
Favorite Quotations from Jesus Calling®
Padded Hardcover

Jesus Calling® for Kids
Hardcover

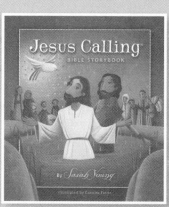

Jesus Calling® Bible Storybook
Hardcover

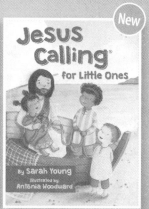

Jesus Calling® for Little Ones
Board Book